✤

# FRANCE, DE GAULLE, AND EUROPE

✤ ✤ ✤ ✤

## THE POLICY OF THE FOURTH AND FIFTH REPUBLICS TOWARD THE CONTINENT

❧

*Other Johns Hopkins Books from*
*The Washington Center of Foreign Policy Research*
*School of Advanced International Studies*

❧

NATIONS IN ALLIANCE:
THE LIMITS OF INTERDEPENDENCE
*George Liska*

THE EXERCISE OF SOVEREIGNTY:
PAPERS ON FOREIGN POLICY
*Charles Burton Marshall*

ALLIANCE POLICY IN THE COLD WAR
*Arnold Wolfers, ed.*

CHANGING EAST-WEST RELATIONS AND
THE UNITY OF THE WEST
*Arnold Wolfers, ed.*

DISCORD AND COLLABORATION:
ESSAYS ON INTERNATIONAL POLITICS
*Arnold Wolfers*

INTERNATIONAL PEACE OBSERVATION:
A HISTORY AND FORECAST
*David W. Wainhouse and others*

CANADA'S CHANGING DEFENSE POLICY, 1957–1963
The Problems of a Middle Power in Alliance
*Jon B. McLin*

FORCE, ORDER, AND JUSTICE
*Robert E. Osgood and Robert W. Tucker*

ALLIANCES AND AMERICAN FOREIGN POLICY
*Robert E. Osgood*

❧

# FRANCE

# DE GAULLE

# AND EUROPE

THE POLICY OF THE FOURTH AND FIFTH REPUBLICS
TOWARD THE CONTINENT

SIMON SERFATY

THE JOHNS HOPKINS PRESS, BALTIMORE

TO MY
MOTHER AND FATHER

# FOREWORD

An important feature of international politics since World War II has been the diminished role of the once-great middle-range states of Europe. In large measure the military balance and the dominant political conflict in Europe have been determined by two superpowers outside Europe. It remains to be seen whether developments like the stabilization of the American-Soviet nuclear standoff, the consolidation of détente, the advance of polycentrism in Eastern Europe, and the growing preoccupation of the United States with Asia will induce or enable middle-range states to regain a paramount position in Europe. But if any European country has tried to enhance its security, status, and influence by means less dependent on the superpowers, it is France. The success or failure of France's foreign policy is therefore important for what it shows generally about the bases of power in contemporary international politics, as well as for what it shows specifically about the position of France in Europe and the world.

In this context Simon Serfaty's analysis of the image and reality of the decline and ascendance of French power since World War II contributes to the Washington Center's effort to reassess the foundations of international politics in the light of the current dynamics of national power and interest. His emphasis on the continuing elements of French policy toward Europe throughout the changing conditions of the Fourth and Fifth Republics enables us to view De Gaulle's performance as part of a larger international drama, which, though less spectacular, will be more significant in the long run.

ROBERT E. OSGOOD
Director, Washington Center of Foreign Policy Research

## ACKNOWLEDGMENTS

I want to record my profound gratitude to Professor Robert W. Tucker of The Johns Hopkins University, for his professional guidance and many personal kindnesses while I was struggling with the dissertation upon which this work is based. I wish to acknowledge with grateful appreciation the talented contribution of Professor George Liska, also of The Johns Hopkins University.

My deep thanks are due to my friend, Kenneth Schlossberg, who edited an earlier draft of the manuscript with great care and insight, to Dr. John J. Weltman, now at Wesleyan University, who read part of the manuscript and made valuable suggestions, and to Tain Tompkins, who gave me additional editorial assistance.

I take particular pleasure in thanking my sister, Reinette, for her confidence and support. My brothers, Mérito and André, also remained unsparing of assistance and generosity. I am most grateful.

The encouragement, advice, and friendship of these good people contributed immeasurably to whatever success I have been able to achieve. The responsibility for any faults or errors which remain is, of course, mine alone.

Simon Serfaty

# INTRODUCTION

After 1945, the striking feature of France's position was her diminished status as a Great Power. In a general vein, her situation was part of the over-all decline of Europe in world affairs. But, more specifically, it was a systematic decline begun during the Napoleonic wars, after which French power was no longer sufficient to undertake a war of conquest against the will of a European coalition. Since the Congress of Vienna in 1815, the French search for security—the *cauchemar des invasions*—came to reflect the defensive posture of a weakened nation, and the nightmare became all the more frightening in the face of the growing potential of a rising Germany. "Who"—warned Talleyrand in 1815—"can foresee the implications of a mass like Germany when its divided elements are stirred up and merged?"

By 1945, Talleyrand's somber predictions had been justified three times, and French policy defined security as safety from Germany. But security alone could not be sufficient for a nation whose most inexhaustible source of power—according to Montesquieu—is the vanity of its subjects. The crucial questions to be answered by France were: How could she be safe and independent? How much independence could a nation, obviously wanting in strength, abandon without irreversibly compromising a world position already shattered?

The declining position of France in the world arena was further enhanced by the apparent collapse of her political institutions. After de Gaulle's withdrawal in January, 1946, France turned against herself as, simultaneously, everyone lamented the loss and contended for responsibility. "There is one great man who is not

available, and there are several average men who are available,"
Georges Bidault commented, upon learning of the General's departure. In effect, there were too many average men available—
in less than fourteen years, the Fourth Republic suffered seventeen
prime ministers who formed twenty-five cabinets. As ministers
came in and went out in rapid succession, general boredom with
politics spread throughout the nation, infrequently but blessedly
relieved by such strong individuals as Pierre Mendès-France.

In May, 1958, the return of de Gaulle to power revived the nation. The General was like the Louis XIV described by Montesquieu in his *Persian Letters*: ". . . a great magician whose dominion extends to the minds of his subjects; he makes them what he
wishes. If he has only a million crowns in his exchequer, and has
need of two million, he has only to persuade them that one crown
is worth two, and they believe it." By checking the decline from
within, the Gaullist government made possible the rise of France
abroad. Yet, these ideas of decline and ascendancy—based on an
image of France far more than on her reality—affected neither the
continuity nor the consistency of France's foreign policy.

Under the Fourth Republic, the problem of the French policy
toward the Continent was posed in terms of *past realities and
present expectations*. The past pointed an accusing finger at Germany and called for a revival of the old policy of security enforced
by an alliance with the Anglo-Saxon power islands of the West.
Present expectations soon came to be expressed in terms of a united
Western Europe which would absorb West Germany and contain
Russian expansion.

Under the Fifth Republic, the problem is posed in terms of
*present realities and future expectations*. The Western Alliance
and a united Western Europe including West Germany exist. But
the expectations of a reunited Eastern and Western Europe parallel
those of a reunified East and West Germany. The question is
raised as to whether it remains possible to speak of Europe in terms
of grandeur and national independence while keeping Germany
politically divided and militarily contained. The European problem is indeed the German problem and Germany—which accelerated French decline—also draws the limits of present French
ascendancy.

# TABLE OF CONTENTS

❧

PART I

❧ ❧ ❧ ❧

# FRANCE DECLINING

❧ ❧ ❧ ❧ ❧

※

CHAPTER ONE

※ ※ ※ ※

## THE POLICY OF SECURITY

※ ※ ※ ※ ※

I

In 1945—as in 1919—the main concern of France was Germany. Three times in seventy years German armies had invaded France, thus transforming Franco–German antagonism into what Salvador de Madariaga has called "one of the psychological laws within the soul of Europe." A nation trying to share the laurels of her allies' victory—for some, an "eclipsed nation"—France was channeling the remnants of her strength into the world without. And once more the world without reflected first and foremost the German threat.

To avoid a recurrence of this traditional problem, and at long last to ensure adequate guarantees against renewed German aggressions, the French policy of security sought three major objectives.[1] First, the creation of an independent buffer state east of the Rhine would endow France with an extra measure of physical security, thus compensating for the lack of natural frontiers between the two countries. Second, a regular system of intervention in the domestic affairs of a decentralized Germany would guarantee against indirect aggression, since it would prevent the resurgence of a hostile German state. Third, the assertion of French leadership on the European continent would leave Germany isolated

[1] The following discussion of France's policy of security is partly indebted to Arnold Wolfers, *Britain and France between the Two Wars* (New York, 1940), pp. 11–28.

and France free to organize European security in terms of her own.

There was little effort, in the years following the war, to debate the *bien-fondé* of a policy which still treated Germany as if she had remained at the center of the world problems.[2] Isolated during the war years, France had lost sight of the tremendous changes which had occurred within the international system and, like most other Western countries, she attempted to correct the old mistakes of 1919 rather than to evaluate the new conditions of 1945.[3] Significantly, nothing close to a program equipped to deal with the necessities of a bipolar world appears in the Gaullist statements following *la faillite* of 1940, and it was not until the Communist aggression in Korea that French diplomacy would fully appreciate the major political upheaval brought about by the emergence of the two Super Powers.

"France is very clear on the problem of the Rhine"—Charles de Gaulle reminded the Allies before the Yalta conference—"the Rhine *is* French security."[4] In effect, this was even truer after Potsdam, when the amputation of Germany's eastern territory displaced the current of German vitality westward and aroused fears that sometime in the future German aggressiveness might face westward too.[5] This concern with a hypothetical German resurgence raised the question of direct aggression or to put it another way, a problem of physical security had to be met with concrete guarantees—that is, a strategic border on the Rhine. The first element of the French thesis on Germany was that France ought to establish herself solidly from one end to the other of the Rhine, on the left bank of which the *zone de securité* required that there should be no further sovereignty of a central German state.[6]

[2] As an exception, see Raymond Aron, *L'Age des Empires et l'Avenir de la France* (Paris, 1945), p. 318.

[3] Barbara Ward, *The West at Bay* (New York, 1948), p. 85.

[4] Quoted in *L'Année Politique, 1944–1945* (Paris, 1946), p. 101.

[5] De Gaulle's interview with *The Times* (London), Sept. 10, 1945. In *Le Salut*, Vol. III of his *Mémoires* (Collection Livre de Poche; Paris, 1959), pp. 224–25.

[6] Charles de Gaulle, *Mémoires*, III, 82.

The possibility of intervening in the domestic affairs of Germany would grant France supplementary guarantees against all forms of indirect aggression. During the existence of the Allied Control Council, French obstruction was aimed at preventing the creation of any central German administrative agency and of any uniform economic plan for Germany as a whole, as envisaged at Potsdam.[7] In the view of the French government, only the absence of tentacular administrations with their own power of decision would preserve the autonomy of each zone, at least until a final Four-Power settlement, along the lines of a division rather than a reunification of Germany, would make it impossible for any central German government to revive its military power.[8] The search for such a final dismemberment of Germany was still strong as late as March, 1948, less than three months before the final agreement in London for the unification of West Germany. "There are several Germanys," said the then Premier Robert Schuman, "so strongly divided by their geographic, ethnic, and economic peculiarities that it would be possible to let them separate and organize into autonomous states. These states could then federate for common and limited tasks. Such is our conception of future Germany." [9]

German dismemberment would provide the basis for French economic security, furthered partly by the dismantling of existing facilities, partly by placing the Ruhr under international control, and partly by joining the Saar with Lorraine. The combined economic resources of these two regions would be a counterpoise to the Ruhr, and, all in all, the economy of Germany would serve the

[7] Sumner Welles, *Where Are We Heading?* (New York and London, 1946), p. 93. The Allied Control Council gave the right of veto to its member. It ceased to function on Mar. 20, 1948, after Soviet Marshal Sokolovsky walked out of the session.

[8] See Bidault's note to U.S. Secretary of State James Byrnes (Mar. 1, 1946). Quoted in Georgette Elgey, *La République des Illusions, 1945–1951* (Paris, 1965), p. 133.

[9] Speech to the National Assembly reprinted under the title "La Situation en France." Excerpts quoted in Edgar S. Furniss, *France, Troubled Ally* (New York, 1960), p. 41.

other powers of Europe and, in particular, France which was afflicted by a serious coal shortage.[10]

"Of course, we do not have the temerity to believe that we can alone assure the security of Europe. We need alliances." [11] International guarantees underwrote the security system France was trying to promote on the Continent. The Moscow Alliance with "the strong and brave Soviet Russia" (December, 1944), and the Dunkirk Alliance with "the old and courageous England" (March, 1947), were complementary to the extent that both singled out Germany as the potential aggressor. As de Gaulle described it, the security of the Old World was to be restored around these three poles: London, Paris, and Moscow.[12] But in order to lay the foundation of a stable security, this almost-revived *Triple Entente* needed better balance within its ranks—a balance which could be reached only through the active participation of the United States in the security system thus being established. France, as self-appointed mediator in the East–West conflict, worked relentlessly for the success of a Four-Power conference where the unity of the former Allies would be renewed on the basis of a general agreement on the German problem, thus giving France the *sécurité totale* which had escaped her in 1919.

These alliances were supplemented by multilateral guarantees. France clearly tried to impose the label of collective security upon the new international organization. She demanded a precise Charter, short in length and specific in its clauses, which would enable the member countries to act effectively in accordance with its essential aims and without pointless and endless discussions over its interpretation.[13] The French government did not favor the veto,

[10] French statements of policy on Germany are quite numerous. See, among many, de Gaulle's *Mémoires*, III, 56–58. In this passage, de Gaulle warns against "*la malveillance des puissances anglo-saxonnes*" which, between the wars, had compelled France—he writes—"to renounce guarantees and reparations." (p. 56)

[11] Charles de Gaulle, speech of Feb. 5, 1945. Quoted in Roy C. Macridis (ed.), *De Gaulle, Implacable Ally* (New York and London, 1966), p. 125.

[12] *Mémoires*, III, 68.

[13] Deputy Foreign Minister Maurice Schumann, Eighth Session of the General Assembly, French Embassy, *Speeches and Press Conferences*, No. 13 (Sept. 25, 1953).

at least in the Security Council, as it was fairly confident of general support against the "non-peace-loving" nations still identified as the Axis powers.[14] And finally, stress was placed upon the need for an enforcement of Article 43 of the Charter calling for the organization of an international force.[15] When it became apparent that law, embodied in the United Nations Charter, would not be backed up by such an international force and that the Security Council had become "an organ of conciliation and mediation far more than . . . a tool of protection and repression"[16] against aggressive nations, subsequent French governments naturally turned toward regional guarantees, arguing that "it is not incumbent upon the U.N. to settle directly . . . regional problems."[17]

All French political parties agreed on the German problem, with the exception of the Socialists. The Socialist party (SFIO), primarily concerned with economic security and still infused with the idea of international nationalization, rejected any dismemberment of Germany or any annexation of territories specifically German. In theory, the Socialists were eager for a closer entente with the British Labour government, whose policy of conciliation they generally endorsed. Nevertheless, in practice the SFIO became captive to the other parties whenever they were included in the government (be it one of Tripartism or of the Third Force).

The Allies were uncertain in their reactions to French fears.

[14] Charles Chaumont, "A French View on Security through International Organizations," *International Organization*, Vol. IV, No. 2 (May, 1950), pp. 236–46.

[15] "Law, embodied in the U.N. Charter, must be backed up by an international force." René Mayer, *Journal Officiel*, Débats Parlementaires Assemblée Nationale (July 22, 1949), p. 5070 (hereinafter cited: *J.O., Deb., A.N.*). In the thirties, de Gaulle, as a governmental official, had carefully studied the plans that were proposed by Tardieu and Paul-Boncour for an international force. He favored them as consistent with France's interest in preserving the status quo. *Vers l'Armée de Métier* (Paris, 1945), pp. 95ff.

[16] Robert Schuman, then Foreign Minister, *J.O., Deb., A.N.* (July 23, 1949), p. 5229.

[17] Pierre Mendès-France, then Prime Minister, at the U.N. General Assembly. French Embassy, *Speeches and Press Conferences*, No. 34 (Nov. 22, 1954), p. 9.

Even after the rupture of the Moscow conference of April, 1947, France still hoped to find in Russia a staunch ally against Germany. The French thought that a community of interests—their mutual distrust of a German revival—existed between France and Russia.[18] Speaking directly to the Russian delegation at the United Nations, Maurice Schumann, then a Deputy Foreign Minister, reminded Russia that "no nation understands better than France what the haunting fear of invasion and the obsessive longing for security can mean."[19] Nevertheless, Stalin's opposition remained constant after de Gaulle's refusal, during his 1944 trip to Moscow, to endorse the Soviet policy in Poland.[20]

The attitudes of Great Britain and the United States were lukewarm, too. Great Britain at first showed a marked tendency toward a complete espousal of the French cause. "I have repeatedly stated," recalled Churchill by the end of the war, "that it is the aim of His Majesty's Government, of . . . Great Britain . . . to see erected once more, at the earliest moment, a strong, independent, and friendly France."[21] The British government, resuming its post–World War I policy, saw in an early reassertion of French leadership on the Continent the best guarantee of a European balance. In fact, it was upon Churchill's insistence that France had been granted a zone of occupation in Germany, and it was also upon his recommendation that President Roosevelt, in his last Message to the Union, fully recognized France's vital interest in a lasting solution to the German problem.[22] But France's repeated use of her veto power at the Allied Control Council, coming after the

[18] De Gaulle was then speaking of a Russia ". . . interested as we are in preventing, in the future, any German threat." Quoted in Joseph Barsalou, *La Mal-Aimée* (Paris, 1964), p. 27.

[19] Address to the Eighth Session of the U.N. General Assembly, No. 13, p. 6.

[20] Stalin tried forcefully to obtain from the French government full recognition of the Dublin Polish committee. De Gaulle, *Mémoires*, III, 78–80 and 83–84.

[21] Great Britain, *Parliamentary Debates* (Commons), Vol. 403 (Sept. 28, 1944), col. 495.

[22] Quoted and commented on by Robert E. Sherwood in *Roosevelt and Hopkins* (New York, 1948), pp. 845–46.

clashes over military strategy which had developed during the closing months of the war, transformed Anglo-Saxon understanding into impatience and, soon, hostility. In effect, the Allies could not forget their surprise and disappointment following the early political collapse, military disaster, and national capitulation of France in June, 1940.[23] As a result, they saw in France an area of weakness, the strengthening of which was a prerequisite to a strong and unified Western policy.

Later in the forties, the French thesis on Germany was altered —not because France changed her aims, but because she was compelled by her very weakness to accept a succession of compromises that emptied it of its substance. Despite Byrnes' assertion at Stuttgart that Germany would never be "a partner or a pawn in a military struggle for power between the East and the West," the emergence of Germany as a major element in the Cold War was unavoidable.[24] After the rupture with Russia, and given the obvious conflict between the French thesis of coercion and the Anglo-Saxon thesis of co-operation, France had to make a clear choice: either to agree, or to disagree, with everybody. Neither option would have given her total security against Germany. But, as we shall see, the multiplication of the *garanties supplémentaires*, together with various developments at home and abroad, convinced her to adapt her views—first on dismemberment, the Rhineland, and the Ruhr, and next on the question of rearmament and the Saar. Until the Geneva Conference of 1955, Germany remained an unsurmountable obstacle to French diplomats—one concession by the Allies to France generally being followed by two concessions by France to the Allies. "It is like a voice crying in the wil-

[23] See the interview of Harry L. Hopkins with de Gaulle. *Mémoires*, III, 97, and Documents, pp. 411–15.

[24] For content and significance of the Stuttgart speech, see James F. Byrnes, *Speaking Frankly* (New York, 1947), pp. 188–91. A few months later, an influential French parliamentarian reflected the mood of the Assembly and the government when he complained that "Germany is becoming for other countries a stake in a gigantic competition from which the will for power is not always excluded." Paul Bastid, *J.O., Deb., A.N.* (Feb. 27, 1947), p. 402.

derness," lamented Foreign Minister Georges Bidault,[25] but neither he nor his partner at the Foreign Ministry, Robert Schuman, could implement his policy over the rising opposition abroad.


## II

The failure of the Moscow conference of April, 1947, and Molotov's rejection there of the French thesis over Germany in favor of her neutralization under Soviet aegis, together with the domestic breakdown of Tripartism after the Communist dismissal from the Ramadier government (May 5, 1947) helped to persuade France to throw in her lot with the West. Her attitude toward Germany reflected a confrontation between the wishes of the National Assembly and those of the Allies. The confrontation was particularly acute over the matter of German rearmament, when France would seek to restore a German force powerful enough to deter and eventually defeat a Soviet attack, yet not sufficiently powerful to endanger her own security.

The London Agreements (June, 1948), which marked the birth of the West German state, and the Occupation Statute (April, 1949), which outlined the limits of its independence, rejected almost all of the major elements of the French policy. The National Assembly, aware that a refusal of either agreement would dangerously weaken the position of France *vis-à-vis* her Western partners whose co-operation was still the safest guarantee, nevertheless expressed dissatisfaction that the London Agreements did not take into account, in many important respects, the French claims.[26] The Rhineland failed to receive any special status. The industry of the Ruhr remained in German hands. Instead of a loose confederation of autonomous German states, a centralized German government was instituted, with police, legislative, and tax-raising

[25] Quoted in *L'Année Politique, 1946*, p. 428.
[26] The London Agreements were ratified by the slim majority of 300 votes against 286.

powers.[27] The Statute itself, rather than being detailed and legal-
istic as the French wanted it, was concise and general, thus leaving
open the possibility of a further extension of Germany's newly
regained independence. But at least the Petersberg Protocol of
November 24, 1949, which recognized West Germany as a peaceful member of the European community, maintained the principle
of demilitarization of the federal territory. These various agreements to which France consented did not mean a change of policy
toward Germany, but the adoption of a new strategy better suited
to the novel conditions prevailing on the international and domestic scenes, particularly the prospects of a united Europe.

The use of the European idea to control Germany represented
a regional adaptation of the reliance upon international guarantees.
During the period between the wars, France had used bilateral
agreements to surround her potential enemy. She would now try
a more global approach: if weakening Germany through dismemberment or absorbing her through annexation were unacceptable
to the Allies, absorption through integration might do. Multilateral security would thus seek "the integration of a peaceful Germany in a United Europe, a Europe in which the Germans . . .
will be able to give up all idea of dominating it." [28] Security was no
longer to be forcefully imposed on the Rhine, indeed it could not
be a matter for one country alone:[29] while the Atlantic community
would protect Europe from without (by balancing Soviet imperialism), the European community was to protect it from within
(by containing German militarism).

It was felt that to integrate Germany in a European community
would—politically, economically, and psychologically—render
impossible any new German aggression. This strategy, supported
by a good deal of long-range confidence in the European spirit,

[27] F. Roy Willis, *France, Germany and the New Europe, 1945–1963*
(Stanford, 1965), p. 23.

[28] Georges Bidault (then Foreign Minister), *J.O., Deb., A.N.* (Feb. 13,
1948), pp. 741–47.

[29] Robert Schuman, quoted in Alexander Werth, *France, 1940–1955*
(New York, 1956), p. 426.

was equally motivated by short-range mistrust in German nationalism. Thus rearming Germany was still out of the question. In the
words of the French Foreign Minister, "the rearmament of Germany cannot be undertaken without a grave mistake and without
France's complicity." [30]

Late in 1949, the possibility of rearmament had already been in
the background of the Allies' negotiations, though it had consistently been denied by all parties concerned.[31] But the Communist
attack in Korea brought it to the foreground, and on July 24, 1950,
John J. McCloy, the U.S. High Commissioner, asked officially that
means of defense be given to the Germans in order to help face
eventual Soviet aggression.[32] On September 11, President Truman
proposed that ten of the sixty scheduled European divisions be
German, while a few days later, NATO members stressed the need
for Germany to participate in the common defense.[33] Agreeable to
the principle of defending German territory, France refused cate-
gorically to rearm it.[34] Yet, five years of stubborn opposition followed by inevitable consent had established such a pattern that
when Defense Minister René Pleven announced his plan for the
establishment of a common European army (on October 24,
1950), it was thought that once more France would accede to the
Allies' demands.

As originally stated, the Pleven Plan did not aim at rearming
Germany.[35] Pressured by the United States and NATO and abandoned by Great Britain, which had at first expressed much aversion
to Germany's rearmament,[36] France sought instead to limit the

[30] Robert Schuman, *J.O., Deb., A.N.* (July 26, 1949), p. 5312.

[31] A good account of the evolution of U.S. thought on the subject of
German rearmament can be found in Lewis J. Edinger, *West German Rearmament* (Documentary Research Division, Air University, 1955), pp. 4ff.

[32] *L'Année Politique, 1950,* p. 168.

[33] *Ibid.,* p. 200.

[34] Final NATO Communiqué in Lord Ismay, *The First Five Years,
1949–1954* (Paris, 1955), p. 168.

[35] The Plan was presented by Mr. Pleven at the National Assembly,
*J.O., Deb., A.N.* (Oct. 25, 1950), pp. 7118–19.

[36] See, for instance, Mr. Bevin's statement in *Parliamentary Debates*
(Commons), Vol. 473 (Mar. 28, 1950), col. 318–30.

scope of such a rearmament by surrounding it with guarantees. Confusion arose, however, from the contradictory attitudes which the subsequent French governments—up to the time of Pierre Mendès-France—had to adopt. To avoid being overthrown, they had to give in to the Assembly; but, to avoid being diplomatically isolated, they also had to give in to the wishes of the Allies. The Allies, who had asked for German rearmament, accepted the Pleven Plan in which they saw an efficient pooling of Europe's military resources. When in turn the French government accepted the so-called Spofford Proposals, they seemingly accepted the American timetable which gave high priority to German rearmament (as opposed to the French timetable, wherein the rearmament of Germany was to be dependent upon the prior creation of a common European army and a common political institution),[37] and it appeared to the Allies that the agreement of France had been definitely secured.[38] Yet René Pleven had made it very clear that his scheme did not imply "directly or indirectly, conditionally or unconditionally" the creation of a German army; and on October 26, 1950, the National Assembly had requested overwhelmingly (402 votes to 168) a similar pledge from the government.

On the other hand the French government, which had offered the Pleven Plan, was given the European Defense Community (EDC)[39] two years later. But the Pleven Plan and the Commu-

[37] Essentially, the Spofford Proposals recommended that the recruitment of West German troops should be permitted for combat groups much larger than envisaged in the original Pleven Plan; German troops were to be formed into units of 6,000 men on the ratio of one German group to five from other participating countries.

[38] Peter Calvocoressi (ed.), *Survey of International Affairs, 1940–1950* (London, 1953), p. 167. From then onward, "Washington, having cold-shouldered the Pleven proposal . . . shifted to the opposite extreme, and came to look upon EDC as the cornerstone of America's European policy." Michael Florinsky, *Integrated Europe?* (New York, 1955), p. 104.

[39] The EDC Treaty was signed by the six participating states on May 27, 1952. Ratified by the parliaments of four of these countries (West Germany, the Netherlands, Belgium, and Luxemburg, respectively in March, July, November, 1953, and April, 1954), it was on the verge of being ratified by the Italian parliament when it was rejected by the French Assembly on Aug. 30, 1954.

nity were two different propositions. Whereas Pleven's scheme called for the fusion of contingents in the smallest possible units, the EDC Treaty asked for such a fusion to be made at a level close to that of a full-strength division. At the same time, the postponement of further debate over the supranational issue (an essential element of the Treaty) made France fear that there would be juxtaposition rather than fusion, thereby making all the more possible an independent revival of the Wehrmacht. The Allies said that there could be no European army divisions without German divisions. The French answered that there could be no European army divisions with German divisions[40]—yet everyone referred to a complete agreement.[41]

Within France, the opposition to the EDC rested on a wide spectrum of reasons. The Communists and the extreme right did not want rearmament of Germany in any form or under any circumstances.[42] The Gaullists were agreeable to the idea, but thought that the EDC represented the worst method, since it would denationalize the French army and implied one more step toward a "Europe of the technocrats." "Europe is a fiction," had warned one of de Gaulle's closest collaborators, Louis Terrenoire, during the debates on the Petersberg Protocols, "and you are going to integrate Germany into this fiction." [43] There were fears, particularly among the Radicals, that the rearmament of West Germany would make her an active participant in the Cold War and lead to

[40] See the press conference held by Jules Moch (then Minister of Defense), at the French Embassy in Washington, D.C., *Speeches and Press Conferences* (Nov. 1, 1950), No. 24.

[41] The Brussels communiqué of December, 1950, for instance, spoke of a "unanimous agreement regarding the part which Germany might assume in the common defense." Quoted in Ernst H. van der Beugel, *From Marshall Aid to Atlantic Partnership* (New York, 1966), p. 268. The circumstances surrounding the original French acceptance of the EDC Treaty are discussed on p. 18ff. and in Ch. IV.

[42] The Communist solution to the German problem was a very simple one: To replace the old Germany by a new, Communist Germany. Cf. Florimond Bonte, *Le Militarisme Allemand et la France* (Paris, 1961).

[43] *J.O., Deb., A.N.* (Nov. 24, 1949), pp. 6251–54.

a destabilizing arms race between the two sections of Germany. The major source of opposition, however, arose over the geographical definition of the Treaty, which limited it to a narrow Continental frame after Great Britain's expressed opposition to joining it. A large number of French deputies, foremost among them the Socialists, were still afraid of a Franco-German *tête-à-tête* where German dynamism would not be balanced by Great Britain. In effect, the motion granting confidence to the government following the debates over the EDC specifically urged the government to obtain the participation of Great Britain.[44]

Despite repeated statements to the effect that Germany has no armaments and will have none, successive French governments recognized the ultimate inevitability of German rearmament. As Premier Mendès-France reminded the French people during the closing weeks of the four-year debate, "the choice . . . is between a rearmament of Germany that we could still supervise, and a rearmament over which we would have no possible control." [45] Here too, the government's policy was twofold: to dispel the domestic opposition by hiding Germany's military recovery in the fashionable blur of Europeanism and supranationality, and to loosen the American pressure by stalling, thereby keeping Germany's rearmament as small and as slow as possible.

There was strong belief in French circles that the Pleven Plan would finally arouse Russian concern over Germany's entry into the Western system of defense and stimulate the Soviets to a lessening of tensions and some diplomatic concessions in Europe or even in Indochina, where French troops were more and more actively involved. Since these plans were seen as a measure of defense against the Soviets, the case for German rearmament would

[44] The motion was passed by a vote of 327 to 287. Among other sources of opposition was, more particularly, the nostalgia of France's independence. Edouard Daladier, for instance, wanted the French government to let the United States play "the German card" so that "even though we have not as yet recovered our power, we would recover our freedom in international politics." (*L'Année Politique, 1952,* p. 309.)

[45] Broadcast to the French people on Aug. 14, 1954. French Embassy, *Speeches and Press Conferences,* No. 29 (Aug. 16, 1954).

then find itself partly pre-empted. Thus, the EDC and the search for a Four-Power conference complemented each other. "We have not stopped waiting for a gesture from the Soviet Union," complained Mendès-France in the aftermath of the EDC debate. The gesture registered, however, was not that expected.[46] In its note of March 10, 1952, the Soviet Union explicitly accepted in principle both the remilitarization and the reunification of Germany, provided that Germany was pledged not to join any alliance aimed at a state which had fought against her during World War II. The neutrality of a reunified Germany was not acceptable to France, which still remembered the models of the Rapallo (April, 1922) or Moscow (August, 1939) Agreements. "The neutralization of a country . . . like Germany"—recalled Foreign Minister Georges Bidault to the NATO Council—"would result in offering [it] to the highest bidder." [47]

Not before the Mendès-France era did the French government try to reconcile the National Assembly and the Western Allies. The Protocol which it presented to the other five European nations at the Brussels conference of August, 1954, asked satisfaction on three major points: (1) the Treaty was to be a complementary organ of the Atlantic Community, itself established for an indefinite duration, and invalidated if the United States and the United Kingdom revised their policy as defined in April, 1954, or if Germany were reunified; (2) the supranational clauses of the Treaty would become applicable only after a probationary period of eight years; (3) the ratio of forces within the European army (fourteen French divisions to twelve German divisions) would be final, and only troops stationed in the cover zones would be integrated.[48]

Given such a Protocol, a treaty would have consecrated the formation of a Continental bloc within which West Germany would

---

[46] See the account of Molotov's interview with Premier Mendès-France, on July 10, 1954, in Pierre Rouanet, *Mendès-France au Pouvoir, 1954–1955* (Paris, 1965), pp. 231–40.

[47] French Embassy, *Speeches and Press Conferences*, No. 9 (Apr. 23, 1953).

[48] A complete text of the Protocol can be found in *L'Année Politique, 1954*, pp. 632–35.

have been submitted to discriminatory treatment. It was not acceptable to the Low Countries, which would rather have turned to a policy of neutrality backed by France and England plus the United States.[49] It was also unacceptable to Germany, whose position was strengthened by the growing impatience of the United States, as well as by the steady hints for reunification which were coming from the East. Moreover, the U.S. administration made it emphatically clear that it could not accept the delays necessary for the renegotiation of a new treaty.[50] But for France the rejection of most of the clauses of her Protocol meant the end of the short-lived search for an alternative to the Treaty of May, 1952. As Mendès-France had warned the Brussels conference, it was to prove fatal. The EDC, which grew out of a concern for national defense and the further containment of Germany, collapsed amidst national division and the Western endorsement of Germany's rearmament.

With the sole exception of the Communists, all parties in France agreed that "the Germans must be integrated in a system of defense, but they must not be granted the possibility of any dangerous initiative." [51] Short of direct participation, such a guarantee was actually underwritten on numerous occasions by both Great Britain and the United States. Mutual assistance was promised through the Assistance Treaty between the United Kingdom and the EDC, and through the NATO Protocol, both signed on May 27, 1952. That same day, the Tripartite Declaration of France, the United States, and the United Kingdom was signed, proclaiming their abiding interest in the effectiveness, the strength, and the integrity of the Community. The same Declaration reaffirmed the willingness of both the United States and the United Kingdom to

---

[49] See Spaak's and Beyen's statements (as Belgian and Dutch Foreign Ministers, respectively), in Rouanet, *Mendès-France au Pouvoir*, pp. 229 and 260.

[50] Dulles' warning of an impending "agonizing reappraisal" was confirmed by the White House press release of Dec. 23, 1953. Quoted in van der Beugel, *From Marshall Aid to Atlantic Partnership*, p. 294.

[51] Edouard Bonnefous, quoted in *L'Année Politique, 1950*, p. 274.

station forces on the continent of Europe, including the Federal Republic of Germany, and was confirmed by the United Kingdom in its Unilateral Declaration of April 13, 1954. Finally, the same Unilateral Declaration reaffirmed co-operation between the United Kingdom and the European Defense Community, while the letter of President Eisenhower to the EDC countries (April 16, 1954) confirmed and restated all previous pledges.[52]

However, the problem, particularly in the case of Great Britain, was that these concessions seemed always to be made—to use Churchill's expression—"in the least possible degree at the latest moment, and in a grudging manner." [53] Nothing short of the formal entry of Great Britain into a community shaped along supranational lines could have erased French fears of being "shut up in a small, dark box," with Germany and without the *Union Française*. A unilateral declaration, even if duly registered, could clearly have no larger scope than that of a unilateral act, and as it had been decreed unilaterally, it could be nullified the same way.

It would be wrong, however, to speak of a diminished enthusiasm on the part of France for Western European unity.[54] At that time, the central issue for France was essentially Germany, particularly following Moscow's tactical shift of pressure to the political level. Western European unity was still regarded as the best possible means for an efficient containment of Germany, provided that three counterpoises to her recovery could be obtained: the formal inclusion of Great Britain, the firm commitment of the United States, and the direct association of the French Empire. Only the latter was adequately obtained, as Churchill—back in power—only agreed that Britain be *with* but not *of* Europe, and John Fos-

---

[52] The texts of these agreements can be conveniently found in the appropriate yearly volume of *Documents on International Affairs*, Royal Institute of International Affairs, London.

[53] Great Britain, *Parliamentary Debates* (Commons), Vol. 469 (Nov. 17, 1949), col. 2222.

[54] Such an interpretation was given by Edgar S. Furniss, "French Attitudes toward Western European Integration," *International Organization*, Vol. 7, No. 2 (May, 1953), p. 199.

ter Dulles periodically threatened France with an agonizing reappraisal of the nature of the U.S. commitment.

In effect, the threat to the security of France was twofold—German militarism and Russian imperialism. The Pleven Plan tried to meet them both simultaneously. On the one hand, a European army would avoid the resurgence of German militarism while taking advantage of the German military potential to help face the Soviet Union. The threat of German rearmament would then serve as added pressure on the Soviets for the gathering of a Four-Power conference where a general agreement would hopefully be reached. The lessening of the Soviet threat, by diplomatic means, would in turn entail the collapse of most of the Anglo-Saxon argument in favor of German rearmament. But still aiming at a new Rapallo—that is, a direct understanding between Russia and Germany—the Soviet Union did not make the kind of concessions expected by France.

The real choice, however, was not a choice of ideals—it was a choice of means. Three levels of reasoning showed that German neo-militarism was necessary to face Russian imperialism. From a military point of view, German territory and German divisions were obviously needed if the Atlantic Community would ever be able to contain the Soviet Army as far east as possible.[55] From a political point of view, a more formal inclusion of Germany into the West would make it more difficult for her to search for alliances eastward. And from an economic point of view, to isolate Germany from a European rearmament would paradoxically contribute to enhancing her position by strengthening her economy, while others would go bankrupt in order to defend her territory and Europe.

The real choice was over the nature of the guarantees surrounding German rearmament. It was the hasty option in favor of a lim-

---

[55] The National Assembly, however, rarely dealt with the military aspect of the issue debated. Cf. Nathan Leites and Christian de la Malène, *Paris from EDC to WEU*, RAND Memorandum, RM/1668/RC (March, 1956), p. 60ff.

ited European framework, rather than an Atlantic one, which had thus been debated. "France is now going through a crisis"—said Robert Schuman to a Harvard University audience—"in the presence of a disciplined and self-assured Germany. She asks herself with genuine and lively concern whether, under the present circumstances, she is able and prepared to face the risks of . . . cooperation on an equal footing with a dynamic Germany, and within a community which Germany, it seems, has a good chance of dominating." [56]

Coming after the rejection by the Assembly of the EDC Treaty, the London and Paris Agreements of October meant a semi-reversion to the Atlantic scheme. Three major concessions were made to the French position. First, a certain level of automaticity was seemingly accepted by the contracting parties who pledged, in the case of an armed attack in Europe, "all the military aid and other aid and assistance in their power." Linked to the provisions of Article 51 of the U.N. Charter on the right to self-defense, such a commitment was even more explicit than that of Article 5 of the North Atlantic Treaty, which had only foreseen such action as the contracting parties deem necessary, including the use of force. Second, Germany agreed to renounce the manufacture on her territory of any atomic, biological, and chemical weapons, long-range or guided missiles, influence mines, large warships, or bomber aircrafts. No other government was required to give an assurance of this kind. It represented, in fact, a broad extension of one of the clauses of the defunct EDC Treaty (Annex II, Part 107). Germany's concession, embodied in a unilateral declaration made at that time by Dr. Adenauer, was further guaranteed by the supervisory powers granted to the Agency for the Control of Armaments (which was also set up by the Agreements).[57] But third and

[56] French Embassy, *Speeches and Press Conferences*, No. 23 (June 11, 1954), p. 8.

[57] Great Britain, Foreign Office, *Final Act of the Nine-Power Conference*, Sept. 28–Oct. 3, 1954 (London: His Majesty's Stationery Office, 1954), Cd. 9289.

foremost, Great Britain at last accepted a quantitative commitment to Europe—four divisions and the tactical air force, or "whatever SACEUR regards as equivalent fighting capacity." Such a physical presence on the Continent could not be reconsidered without the prior agreement of the Brussels Treaty Powers, except in the case of a major crisis overseas.[58] These agreements led to the institution of the Western European Union which, as an extension of the Brussels Treaty of 1948, in its major function as a military organization, became part of the NATO defense system. The admission to NATO of West Germany—now granted "full authority . . . over her internal and external affairs," together with her rearmament, however partly controlled—was now irreversible, and the Saar was the last remaining element of the policy of security.

## III

"If there is one field in which French policy has been well conceived"—stated an outspoken Gaullist critic of the Fourth Republic—"it is the consistency of that policy towards the Saar." [59] This consistency was one of long standing. Three times previously France had seized the Saar territory as a reparation and had made it, at least in part, French territory—between the years 1681 and 1697, 1792 and 1815, and 1919 and 1935. From a strategic point of view, the Saar was a section of a larger buffer zone which France had tried to institute between herself and Germany. The heights overlooking the Saar offered a particularly good natural line of defense on her exposed Northeastern frontier.[60] From an economic point of view, the Saar provided a major interest through its coal

[58] Less than three years later, in 1957, Great Britain withdrew her fourth and last division from the continent.

[59] Michel Debré, *J.O., Deb., Conseil de la République* (Nov. 16, 1950), p. 2933.

[60] On the Saar issue, see particularly Jacques Freymond, *The Saar Conflict, 1945-1955* (London and New York, 1960).

which was an essential complement to the iron ore mines of Lorraine.[61] The main object of France was therefore to devise a formula which would place the economic wealth of the Saar at her disposal and seal its political separation from Germany without jeopardizing the integrity of a territory whose fate, in 1945, was still dependent upon the signing of a peace treaty between the Four Powers and Germany.

During the period 1945–50, the inclusion of the Saar in the French customs and monetary system seemed to provide a *de facto* political detachment from Germany through the emergence of an autonomous and administrative entity whose existence could eventually be recognized in an over-all political settlement.[62] The Allies' agreement, made in exchange for major concessions by France over the Ruhr, served as the final stamp of approval after the breach with the Soviet Union placed her adamant position within the context of a more global opposition.[63]

But the initial success of France's policy arose from approaching the Saar question as an individual problem dissociated (in form if not in fact) from the over-all German issue, thanks to the vacuum of opinion which existed on this question. Besides the Allies— whose first suggestion other than mere endorsement of the French position would not come before the end of 1948 [64]—Germany herself had more urgent problems to solve, such as her monetary reform, the Berlin blockade, and the preparation of a federal constitution, which occupied her during the winter of 1948–49. The following spring, the emergence of the Saar as a separate entity

[61] In 1950, the Saar accounted for 16 per cent of the heavy industrial production of Germany, or 20 per cent of that of France. *L'Année Politique, 1950*, p. 24. See also U. W. Kitzinger, *The Economics of the Saar Question* (Oxford, 1958).

[62] See *J.O., Deb., A.N.* (Jan. 18, 1946), p. 80, a statement of policy made by Georges Bidault. The Preamble to the Saar Constitution, officially proclaimed in December, 1947, was clear in stating the double principle of economic union with France and political detachment from Germany.

[63] See comments made by Byrnes in his Stuttgart speech quoted in *Speaking Frankly*, and by Bevin, *Parliamentary Debates* (Commons), Vol. 423 (June 4, 1946), col. 1845.

[64] Freymond, *The Saar Conflict*, p. 42.

seemed to be furthered by its admission as an associate member to the Council of Europe.

In March, 1950, however, German demands for bilateral negotiations gave the Saar question the status of an intergovernmental conflict. This development introduced a basic contradiction in the position of France: the Conventions signed that year with the Saar had no aim other than to consolidate her status within the framework of the classical policy of the balance of power, whereas the Schuman Plan was designed to lay the foundation for a united Europe. To reconcile these two positions, Robert Schuman and the French government sought to promote the Saar's international personality by granting her sovereignty over foreign affairs (thereby apparently consecrating her independence) and asking for her admission to the European organizations on the same terms as other states (thus promoting new bonds of interdependence).[65] But, by so doing, they merely displaced the emphasis toward another basic contradiction inherent in a policy which included both *présence française* in the Saar and *rapprochement* with Germany. Unable to solve these contradictions, France postponed the diplomatic enforcement of her policy. The Conventions of 1950 emphasized that the newly inaugurated regime of the Saar was temporary only,[66] another way of saying that the Conventions themselves could be modified. Firm as to form, the French position remained prudent as to content.

The uncertainty lying over the relations between France and the Saar was now part of the uncertainty of the relationship between France and Germany, and the fate of French opposition to a return of the Saar to Germany paralleled the fate of her opposition to the rearmament and further reunification of Germany. Here, too, Europeanization was introduced as a means of enforcing Robert Schuman's pledge that "of course, the French will

[65] See R. Schuman's intervention at the Conseil de la République, *J.O., Deb.* (Nov. 16, 1950), p. 2939.

[66] The Convention was very explicit on this point: Freymond, *The Saar Conflict*, p. 73. See also Schuman's statement of Jan. 24, 1950, quoted in *L'Année Politique, 1950*, p. 47.

never accept a pure and simple return of the Saar to Germany." [67]
The problem was now defined in terms of three indissoluble elements: political autonomy, Franco-Saar economic union, European status of the territory.[68] These goals were apparently sal-
vaged by Premier Mendès-France after the rejection of the EDC.
The statute signed in London in October, 1954, placed the Saar
territory under the aegis of the newly created Western European
Union, while retaining the principles covering the Franco-Saar
Customs Union. But when submitted to a referendum, this statute
was refused by a large majority of Saarlanders. Paralleling the issue of German rearmament, the Saar question was settled by new
concessions on the part of France, since the only choice left was to
see the Saar return to Germany with or without her consent.[69]

IV

The weakening of Germany, be it through dismemberment, dis-
mantlement, or any combination of the two, was not, in and of itself, an end to the policy of the Fourth Republic but a means to
the ultimate end which was security. The decade which followed
the end of World War II saw a four-step evolution of this policy.
First, security was sought by the traditional means of limiting Germany's strength. This could be defined as a short-term, unilateral
holding policy. It was associated with determined efforts to contain Germany's potential strength through old-fashioned bilateral
alliances or through international guarantees of collective security.
This was a long-term, multilateral policy of containment. In both
cases, the French government wanted the recognition of existing
facts, aiming at making explicit a situation brought about by Ger-

[67] Quoted in Russell Capelle, *The MRP and French Foreign Policy* (New
York, 1963), p. 64.
[68] Senator Auguste Pinton, Rapporteur of the Foreign Affairs Committee, Conseil de la République, *J.O., Deb.* (Nov. 20, 1953), p. 1871. Quoted
in Freymond, *The Saar Conflict*, p. 151.
[69] The National Assembly approved the ratification of the final settlement by a majority vote of 354 to 225.

many's defeat in World War II. But France's allies were, at the same time, looking forward to negotiating with the Soviet Union with the hope of bargaining about facts, thus somehow *changing* the existing situation. Able to implement neither one of her holding policies, France thus adopted a third approach to the question of security against Germany. Often identified as the Schuman policy, it did not nullify the first two but, in recognition of the declining power of France, it meant to link Germany with other states of Western Europe, to link it organically and not merely contractually, and to do so before the eventual reunification of Germany. This long-term policy of regional integration regarded European integration as another means to ultimate security against a German revival. The Coal and Steel Community, a reformulation of French demands for an International Authority over the Ruhr, was far more acceptable than any military integration in which France would risk her army on the altar of an undefined and uncertain Europe. The ratification of the WEU–NATO agreements further entangled West Germany with Western Europe and the Atlantic Community. For the Soviet Union, as these agreements seemingly closed the Rapallo option, they also made useless any discussion of German reunification.[70] At the 1955 Geneva Summit Conference, the French government was thus satisfied to argue the need for European security in terms of the Soviet requirements, even though some of the military clauses which—according to Edgar Faure—needed to surround a hypothetical reunification of Germany, were identical to some of the guarantees asked by France during the EDC debate.[71] At any rate, convinced that such reunification was postponed *sine die*, the French government could then temporarily break the traditional axiom that the strength of France

[70] See U.S. Department of State, *The Geneva Conference of Heads of Government* (Washington, D.C.: U.S. Dept. of State, International Organization and Conference Series, 1955), Publication No. 6046, Vol. I, No. 29, p. 79.

[71] For example, Edgar Faure suggested that "the whole of Germany, after reunification, must not have forces greater than those held by the present two-thirds of Germany as a member of Western European Union." *Ibid.*, p. 27.

is proportional to the weakness of Germany, now reduced to her Western part. To eliminate West Germany's hostility, thereby putting an end to the historical Franco-German conflict, was the next indispensable goal of the policy of France in Europe. The end of the quarrel, made possible with the settlement of the Saar issue, would finally be formally consummated under the Fifth Republic.

I - weak
II - equality
III - Needed help but was afraid that it would be un equal
IV - Strategy of armament

CHAPTER TWO

# THE ATLANTIC ALLIANCE— THE UNSOLVED TRIANGLE

## I

In 1945, the central question for France was her status. Should she ignore some of the unfortunate events of the war, attempt to remain a Great Power, and "resume the same sort of relations which for several centuries she had had . . . the habit of having with the great nations"? [1] Or, should she instead plainly recognize that too many dissensions, too many diplomatic burdens, and too many wars had made of her a decadent nation?

Obviously, the position of France following World War II was one of extreme weakness. War losses estimated at 4,869 billion francs had brought her near economic ruin.[2] The political reckoning which developed out of the Liberation far exceeded de Gaulle's estimate of "twelve dozens of traitors, twelve hundred of cowards, and twelve thousand of idiots," and further depleted an elite now either dead or discredited.[3] A large part of the French navy had

[1] De Gaulle's speech of Sept. 12, 1944. Quoted by J. B. Duroselle, *In Search of France*, ed. Stanley Hoffmann (Cambridge, 1963), p. 335. See also *Mémoires*, III, Ch. 2.

[2] André Piettre, *L'Economie Allemande Contemporaine, 1945–1952* (Paris, 1952), p. 104. (Figures expressed in 1945 francs.)

[3] Quoted in Jacques Fauvet, *La IVème République* (Paris, 1960), pp. 34–35. According to Fauvet, there were 2,071 death sentences, but twice as many by absentia; 40,000 detentions (2,777 for life), and 48,273 condemnations for national indignities (*ibid.*, pp. 32–33). Official figures given by P. H. Teitgen at the National Assembly on Aug. 6, 1946, reported 4,783 death sentences, 11,000 life sentences, and 19,000 time sentences (quoted in Barsalou, *La Mal-Aimée*, p. 41).

been sunk at Mers-el-Kebir. As to the French Army, it was so poorly equipped that the Allied Command had found it necessary to assign it to the role of maintaining a passive front on the upper Rhine during the last few months of the war.[4] But the French government saw this state of affairs as temporary, a *passagère et partielle défaillance* to be soon overcome.[5] Meanwhile, a policy of prestige could just ignore this lack of power and assume a *de facto* return to normalcy. Thus, the policy of prestige, essentially of a Gaullist origin, described as normal a situation which would preserve for France her Great Power status. Since such status had been acquired by France at the beginning of the modern state system, no other nation could deny it or ask for its further justification without, at the same time, denying the whole history of France.[6] An assumed French tradition of grandeur was thus transformed into a "right to a great place in the concert of people," as a normal place for "a nation which, throughout history, has well served mankind."[7] The direct implications of such a policy, however, were mainly negative, since they implied a code of equality which could not suffer the least rebuke without immediate protest. So the forums of protest would naturally consist of groups in which France felt herself ignored or diminished—the United Nations, as well as the supposed Anglo-Saxon conclave—while she would no less nat-

---

[4] The French frustrations were made evident by the subsequent press comments. "Quite near"—wrote *Combat* on Dec. 23, 1944, at the height of the Rundstedt offensive—"a cruel war is being fought, and we are not allowed to take part in it. The French are not used to being treated as outsiders, as football fans, cheering on the teams." Quoted in Werth, *France, 1940–55*, p. 235.

[5] General Aumeran, *J.O., Deb., A.N.* (Nov. 22, 1949), p. 6158. A typical example of this kind of glorious forecast can be found in this statement by Pierre Mendès-France: "People believed that this country had reached its twilight, its decline. But look at its faith and even its impatience: the wind is rising, morning is here, we are at the dawn of a new France." French Embassy, *French Affairs*, No. 13 (Oct. 5, 1954), p. 6.

[6] Furniss, *France, Troubled Ally*, p. 246. See also André Geraud, "Can France Be a Great Power?" *Foreign Affairs*, Vol. XXVI, No. 1 (October, 1947), pp. 24–36.

[7] Louis Marin, *J.O., Deb., A.N.* (Feb. 27, 1947), p. 484.

urally seek bilateral agreements as the best means of making her voice heard—in Moscow or in Dunkirk. Yet, while led to a policy essentially negative in order to safeguard her rank, France needed, as a consequence of her military decline, to ensure her own security through that of others. A loud "no" as to form was followed in most cases by a discreet "yes" as to content.

The policy of prestige was further rationalized by France's self-description as a keystone of European security and Western defense. Foreign Minister Georges Bidault made it a premise of his policy that "if the European drama . . . can be happily solved, it will have to be with the co-operation of France which, for a long time, has devoted herself to such a task out of duty . . . much more than out of selfish interest." [8] During the parliamentary debates that preceded the vote on the Atlantic Alliance, a French deputy proudly noted: "France is still staggering . . . But without the participation of our country, with its double facade on the Atlantic and Mediterranean, and more than any other nation a trustee of the Western spirit, an Atlantic pact is not conceivable." [9] All in all, then, successive French governments tried to reconcile the compelling necessity of going it with others, and a national desire to go it alone. The problems of promoting security and prestige while facing military and political decline appeared best in the dealings with Great Britain and the United States.

## II

The Marshall Plan was accepted despite fears that it was too intimately linked with the Truman Doctrine. The latter had been regarded by many observers in France as interfering with the political game of every country, inasmuch as the United States was now describing the progress made by the Communist party any-

[8] Georges Bidault, *J.O., Deb., A.N.* (July 26, 1947), p. 3596.
[9] François Quilici, *ibid.* (July 26, 1949), p. 5323.

where in the world as a threat to its own security.[10] As a matter of fact, the announcement of the doctrine had been followed in France by the dismissal of the Communist party from the Ramadier government.[11] Similarly, the Marshall Plan was regarded as a possible infringement on French sovereignty. The bilateral agreement of co-operation signed by the United States and France in June, 1948, contained several restrictive clauses which, according to Alfred Grosser, created a situation somewhat colonialist,[12] as they carried with them conditions committing France to the backing of unpredictable policies of the U.S. government which reserved the right to withdraw its aid from any country not making suitable use of it.[13] France would have liked to obtain the indispensable Marshall aid without having to become a full member of the

[10] See particularly comments made by Raymond Aron in *Combat*, March, 1947. Widely quoted in Werth, *France, 1940–1955*, p. 351. A large fraction of the French Assembly rallied to a similar interpretation and defined the Truman Doctrine as aiming at "opposing any new expansion of the Soviet Union, and even new expansion of communism itself." André Mutter, *J.O., Deb., A.N.* (July 25, 1947), p. 3545.

[11] Actually, it was as much a withdrawal as it was a dismissal. According to Maurice Thorez (then its Secretary), "the French Communist party had to take into account its responsibilities vis-à-vis the international situation." (Quoted in Elgey, *La République des Illusions*, p. 23.) After Bidault's return from the ill-fated Moscow conference, late in April, 1947, the Communist *esprit de corps* made the withdrawal from the French government unavoidable. Ramadier himself has denied that some form of American pressure was behind his dismissal of the Communists (as quoted in Jean-Raymond Tournoux, *Secrets d'Etat* [Paris, 1960], p. 133). Yet, in other instances, he has made himself the obvious connection between the international events of March–April, 1947, and the domestic events of April–May, 1947 (see Barsalou, *La Mal-Aimée*, p. 82, and Elgey, *La République des Illusions*, pp. 277ff.). On this question, see also Jacques Fauvet, *Histoire du Parti Communiste Français*, II (Paris, 1965), 191ff.

[12] *La IVème République et sa Politique Extérieure* (Paris, 1961), p. 221.

[13] Harry B. Price, *The Marshall Plan and Its Meaning* (Ithaca, New York, 1955), p. 22. The main conditions of this agreement are mentioned in Grosser, *La IVème République et sa Politique Extérieure*, pp. 220–21. Pierre-Henry Teitgen would draw the consequences of the U.S. policy when, early in 1947, he advocated the patricipation of the MRP to a coalition government on the assumption that "it is not to a socialist-communist government that the U.S. will consent to loan us the money which we need." Quoted in Jacques Fauvet, *La IVème République*, p. 75.

American welfare office.[14] There was here a gap between the legal France, as embodied by the government's policy of submitting to the impossibility of remaining isolated, and the real France, whose majority still regarded the great schism as a matter of choice between the lesser of two evils.

It is precisely such a choice that the government had tried to avoid through the short-lived experience of international tripartism between 1945 and 1947. Outlined by de Gaulle, then followed by Georges Bidault, international tripartism wanted Europe to be neither a pawn in the game of others, nor their battlefield but instead a link between the two worlds, a link which would ultimately turn into a buffer.[15] Within such a Europe the role of France was —according to de Gaulle—"to persuade the other states bordering on the Rhine, the Alps, and the Pyrenees to join together" into an organization which would become "one of the three planetary powers" and, eventually, "the arbiter between the Soviet and American camps." [16] But Germany was the only cementing factor of such an entente (as it was among the French political parties), and with Great Britain moving closer to the United States position on Germany, and with the Soviet Union making it clear that it would not support the French thesis on Germany either, the future of the revived entente grew dimmer. The liquidation of the Beneš regime struck the death blow, as Czechoslovakia became the symbol of the impossibility of East–West co-existence within a single country. Deserted by the East, France had to move westward, however reluctantly, and to seek a position of equality within the Atlantic triangle, between Great Britain, "jealous in our triumphant days, hospitable in our unhappy ones," [17] and the United States, "located in a different world and whose fate . . . could not be identified with that of Europe." [18]

---

[14] The expression is that of Paul Reynaud, a strong believer in European unity. *J.O., Deb., A.N.* (July 25, 1947), p. 3553.

[15] Speech made by Charles de Gaulle at Brest on July 22, 1944. Quoted in Werth, *France, 1940–1955*, p. 255.

[16] *Mémoires*, III, 211.

[17] Charles de Gaulle, *Vers l'Armée de Métier*, p. 18.

[18] André Passeron, *De Gaulle Parle, 1962–1966* (Paris, 1966), p. 297.

Here too, then, it was less a choice of ideals than a choice of means as the Atlantic triangle rested on a basis of incertitude concerning France's attitude toward her Anglo-Saxon partners as well as toward the Cold War as a whole. The Dunkirk Treaty solved hardly any problems between France and England. It merely postponed them. Both countries expressed their belief that the conclusion of such a treaty would provide the basis for settlement of all problems which could arise between them.[19] Furthermore, an acute rivalry had already developed between London and Paris as to who would assume, *vis-à-vis* the United States, the leadership of Europe. As early as July, 1946, Foreign Minister Georges Bidault expressed his concern that the United States was being incomparably more generous to England.[20] The French passion for equality with Great Britain, certainly enhanced by the anglophile orientation of the U.S. Department of State, was easily understandable, since Great Britain was the only nation with which the concept of equality had any meaning. Demands for equality obviously would have been absurd if addressed to either Super Power; they seemed superfluous with regard to defeated Germany. At any rate, France resented the fact that Great Britain seemed to conduct a more independent foreign policy.[21] But the British held a major advantage over the French: their concern with Communism was in the nature of an external threat, whereas for France it was an internal as well as an external menace. In view of this, the United States expected from the French government a more impressive display of anti-Communism and pro-Americanism which provoked considerable irritation among the French people, a good third of which regarded the United States as the main threat to world peace.[22]

This doubt as to the real nature of the American involvement

[19] For the English text of the treaty, see *Documents on International Affairs, 1947–1948*, pp. 194ff.

[20] Quoted in Werth, *France, 1940–1955*, p. 315.

[21] See Frederick Northedge, *British Foreign Policy, the Process of Readjustment, 1945–1961* (London, 1962), *passim*.

[22] See polls published by the Institut Français d'Opinion Publique, in Philip Williams, *Politics in Post-War France* (London, 1954), Appendix vii, pp. 446–48.

in Europe was particularly widespread among the intellectual and military strata of French opinion. For François Mauriac, for instance, "both technocracies [Russian and American] which believe themselves antagonistic lead humanity toward an identical dehumanization." [23] Such intellectual anti-Americanism, largely based upon widespread feeling that the United States would not be able to fill the ideological vacuum of the West, provoked a strong current in favor of neutrality between both factions since the military rearmament of the West would not make sense if its political disarmament subsists.[24] Among the general public, this neutral current was further enhanced by a variety of fears: fears of Communist riots, of the new military technology, of Russia, and of Germany, together with a growing skepticism shared by many French generals over the efficacy of the mechanics of alliances and armies.[25] The point here is that despite official denials and the impossibility—repeatedly stated by governmental sources—of neutralism exercising any important effect on France,[26] these fears and reservations remained in the background, finding novel expressions after each pronouncement that would seem to present an offensive character—Dean Acheson's "negotiations from strength," Truman's "total diplomacy," or Dulles' "roll-back policy."

The Atlantic triangle was the outcome of a choice of means, we have said, but the means themselves were not regarded as ideal. Georges Bidault best expressed the mood of the National Assembly when he described the North Atlantic Pact as "not the result of enthusiasm . . . but the fruit of a very grave disappointment and . . . a very heavy fear." [27] The disappointment was the fail-

[23] Le Figaro, Feb. 20, 1950. Quoted in L'Année Politique, 1950, p. 69.
[24] Maurice Duverger, Le Monde, Aug. 23, 1950. Quoted in L'Année Politique, 1950, p. 179.
[25] For example, see General Billote, Le Temps du Choix (Paris, 1950).
[26] In 1951, for example, Vincent Auriol, then President of the Republic, described neutralism as "always alien to the French soul, not only because it is a moral absurdity, but because it is an historical and geographical nonsense." Quoted in L'Année Politique, 1951, p. 92.
[27] J.O., Deb., A.N. (July 26, 1949), p. 5302.

ure to stimulate a Four-Power understanding (particularly since it would have been based on Germany) and the fear related to the apparent intensification of the Cold War.

For the French Communist party, the Atlantic Pact signified the formation of a new Holy Alliance directed against Communism and its main sponsor. This newly created "gendarme of the Marshallized world," [28] they argued, would definitely close the door to further negotiations between the East and the West and aggressively freeze the division of Europe into two blocs, in absolute contradiction to the principles of international co-operation pledged in the United Nations Charter.[29]

If we except the Communists, however, the position adopted by the National Assembly toward the Atlantic Alliance was generally favorable. Forceful opposition to the treaty itself was confined to a few self-identified neutralists who saw in it the resumption of the alliance system of pre-World War I and the beginning of a new arms race.[30] All other groups endorsed the treaty as a necessary defensive alliance. But their endorsement was given à contre-coeur, as the French Assembly bitterly criticized the fluidity of the commitment which was submitted to it for approval.

The need for security was obviously the main justification of the North Atlantic Alliance. For the last thirty-five years, French diplomacy had sought an alliance of this sort, an alliance which would finally entangle Great Britain and the United States on the Continent, thus transforming European security into a matter of interest to both sides of the Atlantic. The French government put its case to the National Assembly in a most succinct form: "We have today obtained what we had hoped for in vain between the two wars: the United States recognizes there is neither peace nor security for America if Europe is in danger." [31] But the French government also wanted to make it clear that the American entan-

[28] Jacques Duclos, *ibid.*, p. 5339.
[29] See, more particularly, Pierre Cot's intervention, *ibid.* (July 23, 1949), pp. 5307–11.
[30] Paul Boulet, *ibid.* (July 25, 1949), pp. 5231–33.
[31] *L'Année Politique, 1949*, p. 54.

glement in the affairs of Europe was not merely confined to opposing the Soviet Union and the spread of Communism. Instead, the French emphasized the general nature of the new alliance: "The pact is directed against no nation, or group of nations but against any aggressor whoever it is." [32] The Assembly itself was still more specific than the government, and it warmly endorsed René Mayer's remark that "NATO is directed against any aggressor . . . Germany included." [33]

This concern with Germany did not preclude the National Assembly from seeking security from the Soviet Union as well. But while France always seemed to assume an innate German aggressive instinct, she attributed to Russia weak aggressive designs combined with a strong defensive complex. In view of this, the French government was anxious to emphasize the defensive nature of the North Atlantic Treaty. Neither the United Nations, rendered powerless by the veto system and the failure to implement Article 43 calling for the establishment of an international force, nor direct collaboration with the Soviets, rendered futile after the fruitless conferences of 1947, nor general disarmament, made utopian by too many years of negative discussions, could guarantee the safety of France. Far from freezing the developing Cold War, the Atlantic Alliance would open channels for future negotiations which would hopefully emerge out of the military stalemate thus being created. And if there were ever to be discussions with the Soviet Union, the task of the French government was to ensure that they would not be limited to the two Super Powers.[34] At the same time France was bound to concede that she alone, in an obvious position of military weakness, could not initiate such negotiations since —if things came to the worse—she could not defend herself for a very long time.[35]

[32] Robert Schuman, *J.O., Deb., A.N.* (July 25, 1949), p. 5228.
[33] René Mayer, *ibid.* (July 22, 1949), p. 5068. The concern with Germany was most forcefully expressed in the presentation of Pierre Montel (*rapporteur* for the Committee on National Defense), whose three sons had been killed by the Germans during World War II.
[34] Georges Bidault, *J.O., Deb., A.N.* (July 26, 1947), p. 3596.
[35] René Mayer, *ibid.* (July 22, 1949), p. 5070.

The question of the compatibility of the Atlantic Alliance with other major international agreements subscribed to by France was twofold, as it involved both the Franco-Russian Alliance and the United Nations. In the former case, the issue was brought about not only by the Communists but also by a large fraction of the Assembly, which was afraid that an enforcement of a Pax Americana would offend sensitive Russian reflexes. As Article 5 of the Moscow Treaty of 1944 pledged the contracting parties "not to conclude any alliance or take part in any coalition directed against either party," the question was to assess whether the Atlantic Pact was in fact primarily directed against the Soviet Union. The treaty itself stated (Article 8) that "none of the international engagements now in force between [each party] and . . . any third state is in conflict with the provisions of this treaty." This was in line with the view of the French government which, as we have just seen, defined the main target of the new alliance in terms of the permanency of the German danger.[36] In fact, the case could even be made—and it was—that to the extent that the Atlantic Alliance was directed against Germany, it represented a useful complement to the Franco-Russian Alliance.[37] At any rate, it was clear that the French government was eager to protect the agreement of December, 1944. "France," declared Robert Schuman, "still regards herself as bound by the Franco-Russian treaty." [38]

Already, under the League of Nations, the debate over the compatibility of a regional organization with a system of collective security had been raised when France tried to supplement the League with the Little Entente and other bilateral agreements. Even though the League of Nations made only brief reference to regional understandings (Article 21), France had concluded a series of regional pacts on the assumption that these, far from weakening the League structure, would be a source of strength since they would provide the League with a sound underpinning of lim-

[36] André Mutter, *J.O., Deb., A.N.* (July 25, 1949), p. 5226.
[37] P. O. Lapie, *ibid.*, p. 5235.
[38] Robert Schuman, *ibid.*, p. 5229.

ited military obligations apt to reinforce its commitment to the preservation of order.[39]

In the case of the United Nations, the issue at stake was more or less identical. It was pointed out that the Charter expressly rules out action under regional arrangements to deal with threats to the peace, breaches of the peace, or acts of aggression (Article 53), except when so ordered by the Security Council which holds primary responsibility for the maintenance of international peace and security (Article 24). Yet, such reasoning was fallacious, inasmuch as it failed to emphasize that on the one hand, the projected alliance could not be regarded as a regional agreement within the meaning of Chapter VIII of the Charter, and, on the other hand, that Article 53 does not take away the right of collective defense under Article 51 for members of a regional agreement.[40]

In effect, what Article 53 forbids is for a regional arrangement to take any enforcement action without the authorization of the Security Council. But the Atlantic Pact mentions only the possibility of self-defense and, for obvious reasons, measures of self-defense, whether individual or collective, do not require any prior authority from the Security Council which only requests that they be immediately reported (Article 51), a pledge actually made by the North Atlantic Treaty.

Finally, the French Assembly and the government criticized the absence of automaticity and uniformity from the Treaty. Nothing in Article 5 suggested that military action would automatically be taken by the United States and Great Britain should Western Europe be invaded; instead both countries, as well as the other member states, merely pledged "such action as [they] deem necessary, including military action." Such a formulation made possible a certain amount of doubt, and it was explained in terms

[39] Grayson Kirk, "The Atlantic Pact and International Security," *International Organization*, Vol. III, No. 2 (May, 1949), pp. 239ff.

[40] Norman J. Padelford, "Regional Organization and the United Nations," *International Organization*, Vol. VIII, No. 2 (May, 1954), pp. 203–16. See also W. Eric Beckett, *The North Atlantic Treaty, the Brussels Treaty and the Charter of the United Nations* (London, 1950).

of parliamentary procedures. While regretting that the proposed alliance was not an unconditional military alliance, the French government suggested that there was still a definite commitment to act, at least in the spirit, if not in the letter of the Treaty.[41] But the spirit of the commitment itself was not based only on the "commonalities" which bound the various nations of the Atlantic Community and the free will to help one another. The North Atlantic Alliance was imposed, in the view of the French government, by the "need . . . to reach an agreement on a common problem," [42] although it was not anxious to define the nature of this common problem as it tried to satisfy simultaneously those who spoke of it in terms of Germany, Russia, or both.

It was also recognized that the Pact itself would not fill the power vacuum then existing in Europe without a rearmament, for which American aid was an indispensable prerequisite. The French Assembly was concerned over the fact that, here too, there was no formal pledge embodied in the Treaty. In the name of the Radical party, Paul Bastid emphasized that "the Atlantic Pact will draw its value primarily out of the American program of armament . . . which is its necessary complement." [43] But to what extent could France depend upon the capricious mood of the U.S. Congress? Lastly, the North Atlantic area itself was criticized as insufficiently broad for not covering the French colonial territories with the exception of Algeria. For France, actively involved in Indochina, a Pacific pact was perhaps more vitally needed than an Atlantic pact, and André Mutter asked that one must be followed by the other.[44]

France expected, moreover, the recognition of her Great Power status through the actual recognition of an intrinsic equality between herself and the Anglo-Saxon countries. While temporarily granting to the United States a position of arbiter, the Assembly

[41] René Mayer, *J.O., Deb., A.N.* (July 22, 1949), p. 5067.
[42] Robert Schuman, *ibid.* (July 25, 1949), p. 5230.
[43] *Ibid.*, p. 5245.
[44] *Ibid.*, p. 5225.

expected that a rapid implementation of Article 9 (which called for the establishment of common institutions), would enable France to be heard at all levels, particularly in the determination of a common defense strategy.[45] While the security of France could ultimately be guaranteed by the Allies' military power, the modalities determining the preservation of such security was a common concern into which the French government wanted to be entered as an equal. In other words, France found in her direct involvement on the Continent a balance between her own risks on the one hand and the military efforts of her allies on the other. A few months after these debates, the Gaullists strongly requested that French obligations and responsibilities in the international strategy foreseen by the Atlantic Pact be formally fixed in a precise and written manner.[46] The Gaullists themselves, then, were most eager to see the pledges made in the Alliance embodied within the formal organization which was to become NATO.

This passion for equality also intended to prevent an uneven distribution of military labor which would grant air and naval duties to the United States and Great Britain respectively while France would man the ground forces. In its report, the Committee on National Defense expressed the hope that France would not accept being the infantry of the coalition, as the preservation of a tactical autonomy was deemed particularly essential to French interests outside the area of the Alliance (in the French Empire).[47] In short, and as seen by the National Assembly, the Atlantic Alliance was too weak in its strong goal (European security), and too strong in its weak goal (military co-operation), since it did not do enough for European security but did too much by seemingly limiting the scope of French activities to Europe only.

[45] Pierre Montel, *J.O., Deb., A.N.* (July 22, 1949), p. 5071.
[46] Gaston Palewski, quoted in *L'Année Politique, 1951*, pp. 89–90.
[47] Pierre Montel, *J.O., Deb., A.N.* (July 22, 1949), p. 5073.

## III

The real nature of the debate over the North Atlantic Treaty was twofold: Would it strengthen France and Western Europe? Would it bring about an improvement of the East-West conflict? Because no satisfactory answer could be given to either of these questions, and because no alternative could be devised either, the pact was accepted by France as the best of the worst systems.[48]

In regard to the Treaty itself, it was expected that a higher level of automaticity could be obtained through the organization of the machinery foreseen by Article 9—an expectation made all the more acute as the Pact seemed to free Great Britain from the automaticity implied in the Brussels Alliance.[49] The Assembly and the government were both aware that without strong alliances, France stood powerless in Europe. "Let us have no illusions"—stated Jean Bouhey speaking for the Socialists—"our army, our navy, our air force . . . are not worth much any longer." [50] France saw in the Alliance a means of recovering, at the least cost, Great Power status.[51] However, the problem remained that by creating the machinery requested by France and her European partners, the United States was building a quasi-permanent system of intervention into European affairs, so that the integrated military alliance necessary in the name of France's security could at the same time mark its irreversible fall from world power.

Actually, this was not the only contradiction existing between the French and American interpretations of the North Atlantic Treaty. In the initial phase of the alliance, the French thought that they were getting a joint military machine that would even-

[48] Georges Gorse, *ibid.* (July 26, 1949), p. 5327.

[49] As in the Franco-Russian Pact, the Dunkirk Treaty—military before all—was applicable in case Germany would adopt an aggressive policy or would merely seem to take initiatives likely to threaten European security.

[50] *J.O., Deb., A.N.* (July 26, 1949), p. 5267.

[51] Robert E. Osgood, *NATO, The Entangling Alliance* (Chicago, 1962), p. 31.

tually come to rest upon the two pillars of automaticity (through military integration) and equality (through full participation in the process of decision-making). But in its original formulation, the Treaty was seen by Washington as a political, rather than a military, obligation—or, as Robert E. Osgood called it, a guarantee pact.[52] It was hoped that the shield provided by the American guarantee would serve to inhibit further Soviet expansion and provide the Europeans with enough time to restore their self-confidence, pursue their national convalescence and ultimately to regain their military stature.[53] Perhaps less inclined to such optimism as to Europe's ability to recover rapidly from the war, the French wanted the Atlantic Alliance to consecrate the restoration of the balance of power in Europe. They expected local defense, as far east as possible, without solving the contradictions between declared strategic objectives and actual capabilities.[54]

The British had been prompt to notice these contradictions. "The foundation and the blueprints are now in," Brigadier Head had said during the debates at the House of Commons, "but there are no bricks for the walls . . . Apart from the atomic bomb, there is in Western Europe today a complete power vacuum; there is practically nothing in the way of a Western European defense organization or defense force which could at present give any security or safety to Western Europe." [55] But what would be the constituents of such power? For France, United States power would suffice, as the defense of Europe was to be based upon "a strategic co-ordination engendered by military agreements guaranteeing to Europe the use of all American forces"—atomic forces first and foremost.[56] The North Atlantic Treaty was thus interpreted as some form of military Marshall Plan in which the Europeans themselves would decide the importance of the aid needed,

[52] *Ibid.*, p. 35.
[53] George Kennan, *Russia, the Atom and the West* (New York, 1958), pp. 89–91.
[54] Osgood, *NATO*, p. 45.
[55] Great Britain, *Parliamentary Debates* (Commons), Vol. 464 (May 12, 1949), col. 2046–47.
[56] Edmond Michelet, *J.O., Deb., A.N.* (July 26, 1949), p. 5272.

which would then be drawn from all American forces pooled for their convenience. But on January 27, 1950, Truman approved the NATO plans for an integrated defense of the North Atlantic area by emphasizing that it provided "for a common defense based on the co-operative use of national military resources and on individual national specialization." [57] This latter concept, however, had been forcefully rejected by the French Assembly as well as by the government. Jules Moch, then Defense Minister, had often stated that "it is out of the question for us to accept a French infantry, a British navy, and an American air force." [58]

The French were thus faced with the dilemma of reconciling decline to grandeur by rallying to the need of going along with others while pretending to retain the ability of going it alone. At first glance, the Alliance would free France from the continual obsession of her isolation. But still, the guarantee pact idea was not desirable because it lacked automaticity and effectiveness in defense and sacrificed the concept of equality among the member states. Yet integration, thereby implicitly demanded, meant diplomatic subordination to Washington and military specialization along Truman's guidelines—both unwanted in the name of French prestige. In the last analysis, only a formal American commitment to massive retaliation against *any* violator of the European status quo could have satisfied France.

Seen in retrospect, it is perhaps unfortunate that these basic differences, which existed between France and her partners from the start, were lost for the public amidst the verbiage of official greetings and final communiqués, as a conscious effort was made to project the image of a fully monolithic bloc. As noted, "to the outsider it sometimes seemed that each new meeting in the North Atlantic Organization produced the same accord that had already been reached a dozen times before." [59] Instead, all that could be said was that during the nascent phase of their co-operation, the members of the Atlantic Alliance certainly agreed on their basic

[57] Quoted in *The U.S. in World Affairs, 1949* (New York, 1950), p. 143.
[58] *L'Année Politique, 1950*, p. 180.
[59] *The U.S. in World Affairs, 1950*, p. 126.

aims: first, to build up defense forces to a sufficient level of strength; second, to devise a common defense strategy; and third, to preserve the sound and stable economy necessary to support such a defense effort.[60] But they remained strongly divided on the best means to fulfill these aims.

The other issue at stake was that of the Cold War. Not just the Atlantic Alliance, but the whole United States policy in Europe, had been criticized in France on the basis that it tended to freeze the East-West split by concentrating on ideological questions instead of promoting a *rapprochement* through the use of the traditional diplomatic methods.

The Marshall Plan itself had not escaped attack. In the motion following a long debate over its approval, the National Assembly had asked for a tight collaboration with *all* European nations and had warned against the threats inherent in the creation of two antagonistic blocs which the Assembly found implicit in Marshall's proposal.[61] Comments of this type were received with impatience on the other side of the Channel and across the Atlantic. Referring to the fact that Marshall's offer was addressed to the whole of Europe, regardless of Eastern and Western considerations, and contrasting it to the skepticism manifested by France and other nations, Foreign Minister Bevin complained that "when the United States throws a bridge to link East and West, it would be disastrous, for ideological or other reasons, to frustrate the United States in this great endeavor." [62] The facts, as they came to be known, indicate that the United States did not expect Russia to participate, and if she should have accepted, she would have been asked as a *donor* country—an invitation unlikely to have gained Russian acceptance.[63] Yet, the Soviet Union was not the

[60] Ottawa Meeting of the Atlantic Council, September, 1951. *The U.S. in World Affairs, 1951*, p. 357.

[61] *J.O., Deb., A.N.* (July 26, 1947), p. 3611.

[62] Quoted from a speech at a meeting of the Foreign Press Association (June 13, 1947), in Ernst H. van der Beugel, *From Marshall Aid to Atlantic Partnership*, p. 58.

[63] Price, *The Marshall Plan*, p. 24.

primary goal of the U.S. Policy Planning staff, which requested that "American effort in aid to Europe . . . should aim . . . not to combat Communism, but the economic maladjustment which makes European society vulnerable [to it]." [64] The choice, however, was between trying to preserve a façade of unity while keeping Europe in "hunger, poverty, deprivation, and chaos," or to accept the split as inevitable and concentrate on Western European and Mediterranean countries. This is, to some extent, the conclusion reached by Hans Schmitt: "Thus the Marshall Plan divided Europe after all. But evidence does not point an accusing finger at the United States. Europe needed help." [65]

After the events which followed the Marshall proposal—among others, the creation of the Cominform, the coup in Czechoslovakia, and the Berlin blockade—it is difficult to understand the renewal of a debate of this type. By then, the East-West split was a *fait accompli* merely acknowledged by the creation of the Atlantic Alliance. But France was still reluctant to be enclosed in the Atlantic triangle, and in her attempt to bring back the fourth Russian partner, she was trying very hard to complete the square.

## IV

The period 1950–1954 is known in France as that of *immobilisme* in domestic as well as in foreign affairs. Each year is a year of transition, though no one knows toward what ends. Korea, which introduced France to the aggressiveness of Soviet expansionism, Indochina, more costly every year, and the EDC, in which France tried to fence in "the German tree," all compelled successive French governments to co-operate with Washington as best as they could.

The Korean conflict brought about a shift of emphasis from the political to the military, as the Communist attack was seen

[64] Memorandum from the Policy Planning staff (May 23, 1947). (Quoted in *ibid.*, p. 22.)
[65] *The Path to European Union* (New York, 1962), pp. 21–22.

as a prelude to a wider offensive against Western Europe. Re-armament became the official doctrine of the Atlantic Alliance. In his June, 1950, Message to Congress, President Truman emphasized its urgency, particularly with regard to the Continent: "The military establishments of Western Europe," he declared, "are below the minimum level consistent with security. Those countries must build up their forces as swiftly as their resources permit, assisted by such help as we can afford." [66] Despite the few non-Communist voices raised at the Assembly claiming that the Korean War had in effect been instigated by the United States to promote European rearmament,[67] the French government rallied to Truman's view and pledged to modernize and re-equip the existing five French divisions, to which would be added fifteen more at an estimated cost of $5.7 billion.[68] This pledge and subsequent pledges of this nature were based upon three conditions. First, the French government wanted the primacy of economic and social factors to be recognized by the Allies. Furthermore, all financial resources were to be gathered in an "Atlantic pool," in which France would occupy a privileged position due to the damages suffered during World War II. Second, all armament would be standardized and its manufacture undertaken by each country according to its particular skill. Third, American and British forces in Europe were to be substantially reinforced.[69]

French promises were obviously overstated. Only a few years before, the authors of the Monnet Plan had bluntly declared that there could be no question of reconstituting a powerful army before preliminary steps had been taken for endowing the country with a modern industrial potential. Furthermore, while the re-creation of the French army was hampered by economic conditions, it was made less possible by the Assembly where, during the early years of the Fourth Republic, there persisted a bitter

[66] Quoted in *The U.S. in World Affairs, 1950*, p. 131.

[67] Jacques Fauvet, *La IVème République*, p. 168.

[68] *New York Times*, Aug. 8, 1950.

[69] First French memorandum on the question, Aug. 5, 1950. Quoted in *L'Année Politique*, 1950, p. 181. Second Memorandum, October, 1950, quoted in *ibid.*, p. 221.

clash between the diverging conceptions of how military strength should be developed and organized.[70] The only possible compromise was to allow the General Staff to dole out penury, in the total absence of general directives or any long-term guidelines. In June, 1949—a year before the outbreak of hostilities in Korea—Paul Ramadier, making a qualitative assessment, admitted that France had "outmoded and outdated materiel which entails excessive maintenance costs."[71] Before him, Gaston Deferre, in the early phase of his political career, had warned that "a ruined France cannot afford the luxury of a great army."[72]

Nevertheless, French promises to the Atlantic partners were necessary. First (and because of conditions already described),[73] France felt obligated to a display of good will toward the United States. René Pleven, then Prime Minister, emphasized that it was France and not England which had been the first NATO member to make a definite commitment to the Atlantic forces.[74] In return for such good will, but before any real commitment, Mr. Pleven expected more economic, military, and political aid. Furthermore, his government expected that a direct relationship would be established between its pledges (on paper) and the American and British commitments (in actuality), since France promised her divisions would permanently constitute half of the total number of European and U.S. divisions stationed in Germany.[75] Second, France wanted to convince her allies that Europe could be defended without German soldiers, so her military contribution must suffice for both France and Germany. Finally, greater French

[70] Paul-Marie de la Gorce, *The French Army* (New York, 1963), p. 339. See also Donald Harvey, "Contemporary Concepts of French Strategy," in Edward Mead Earle, *Modern France* (Princeton, 1951), pp. 421–32.

[71] *J.O., Deb., A.N.* (June 16, 1949), p. 3431.

[72] Quoted in Jacques Fauvet, *La IVème République*, p. 71.

[73] See above, pp. 40–41.

[74] Speech delivered by Mr. René Pleven, French Premier, at the National Press Club in Washington, D.C., Jan. 30, 1951. French Embassy, *Service de Presses et d'Information*, No. 34, p. 2.

[75] Press Conference held by Jules Moch, then Minister of Defense, in Washington, D.C., Nov. 1, 1950. French Embassy, *ibid.*, No. 24, Nov. 2, 1950.

commitments to the defense of Europe would entail more American aid to Indochina. Obviously, at a time when the French position on the Indochinese peninsula was already beginning to look militarily hopeless, Korea provided the French government with a good opportunity to raise the international status of Indochina and to present it, in the words of General de Lattre de Tassigny (then commander of the French troops), as "the same war against the same enemy, for the same cause and at the same price of the same sacrifices." [76]

The actual rearmament of France, however, could not keep pace with the repeated declarations of intention. By the end of 1952, the French ground forces in Europe amounted to twelve-and-one third divisions, considerably short of the scheduled twenty.[77] The shortage was mostly explained in economic terms. In the early fifties, the major French theme was that the Alliance needed not only the security but also the economic equilibrium of the Atlantic community.[78] This principle was easily accepted by the NATO partners, who reversed the question by debating whether or not French contributions to the Atlantic effort exceeded her financial means.

Relative to her national income and budget, France was spending more than her European allies. For 1951, French military expenditures amounted to 740 billion francs or $2,114,000,000 —that is, 13 per cent of her GNP and 34 per cent of her budget— as compared to 9.7 per cent and 33 per cent for Great Britain, and 7.7 per cent and 30.7 per cent for Italy, respectively. The 1951 military budget favorably compared with those of 1948 (before the signing of NATO), 1949 (before its ratification), and 1950 (after its ratification) which amounted respectively to 321 billion, 388 billion, and 420 billion francs.[79]

Yet, the reasons for failure to rearm at a more rapid pace were economic in appearance only. First of all, the increase just men-

[76] French Embassy, *ibid.*, dated Sept. 20, 1951, p. 2.
[77] René Pleven, *J.O., Deb., A.N.* (Jan. 27, 1953).
[78] Hervé Alphand, quoted in Ismay, *NATO*, p. 41.
[79] French Embassy, *French Affairs*, No. 73 (Mar. 17, 1952).

tioned was largely due to the escalation of the conflict in Indochina, which represented almost one-third of the military budget
of France. Furthermore, the core of the effort, during the second
half of 1950 and throughout 1951, was made possible by the end
of the post-war inflation (early in 1949), as the level of prices and
the size of the budget had remained relatively stable during the
eighteen months preceding the outbreak of the Korean War.
Granted that the propensity of France to rearm was economically
limited, the reasons not to rearm within those limits were primarily
political. The French government viewed conventional forces as
the price of admission to the American nuclear guarantee, and
naturally, wanted that price to remain as low as possible. But more
important than the matters of economic bargaining and political
bickering was the point that by denying her full contribution of
ground forces, France left the United States, which was herself
short in such forces, no choice other than nuclear retaliation.

The French government, like most other Western European
governments, understood deterrence in terms of U.S. nuclear
superiority. Conventional forces would increase the chances of
war on the European continent by diminishing the credibility of
American nuclear commitment. Understandably, France refused
to raise an army in the service of a strategic concept that was
adverse, in her judgment, to her national interest. The so-called
peripheral strategy—mentioned in some Allied circles—was particularly attacked since it seemed to endorse the triad of invasion,
occupation, and liberation. Speaking at Bruges in February, 1951,
de Gaulle—as always most outspoken on the issue—condemned it
as "a common strategy which would really hold only peripheral
bastions such as Spain and England, after fighting a few delaying
battles on the Elb, the Rhine, and the Loire, and with the intention
of later liberating the lost ground by destroying everything." [80]

Instead, France recommended the Continental strategy which
would assure her defense as far east as possible, thus making of
Germany the first battlefield of any conflict-to-be. The French
government asked for a "cruising system" whereby the defense of

[80] Quoted in *L'Année Politique, 1951*, p. 52.

Europe would be based on powerful firing fronts constituted "when needed at the right time and in the right place." [81] In other words, the NATO conventional forces—the shield, dear to American strategists—needed to be large enough to prevent a sudden jump by the Soviets across the battlefield countries of the East, but small enough to convince them that should they overrun Germany, nuclear retaliation would be their only reward. The size of the shield thus depended upon the magnitude and urgency of the Soviet threat. When these diminished, the interest of France in the shield declined, as complete reliance was placed upon the United States sword, thereby paving the way for the French "new look" of 1957–58, which signified not the return to the shield, but strong demands for an independent nuclear sword.

[81] René Pleven, French Embassy, *French Affairs*, No. 7 (February, 1954), pp. 1–2.

# CHAPTER THREE

# THE EUROPEAN VOCATION—
# THE UNCERTAIN POLICY

*[handwritten: France tries to form one Europe]*

## I

One of the most acute observers of the French political scene has remarked that the whole European policy of France was merely an accident, based upon an idea which had "neither the transcendence of Messianic ideologies nor the imminence of concrete patriotism." [1] In another instance, the same observer complained that "so much has been said about Europe that one does not know any longer what it is all about." [2] Such confusion is due primarily to different meanings which opposing groups with conflicting aims have placed upon Europe at different times. Besides the extremes of its political spectrum, there were, during the Fourth Republic, three currents of opinion on the European situation, each representing a definite minority. The nationalists (Gaullists and a minority of Moderates) regarded European unification as an idle dream. Instead, they asked for a united Europe which, built on properly elected governments responsible to their national parliaments, would find its reality out of its political content. In contrast to the nationalists, the Europeanists supported unification but were divided into two groups—minimalists and maximalists. The minimalists (mostly Socialists and a few Radi-

---

[1] Raymond Aron, *The Century of Total War* (Paris, 1954), p. 316.
[2] Aron *et al.*, *L'Unification Economique de l'Europe* (Neuchatel, 1957), p. 1.

cals) were willing, under certain conditions, to go beyond national sovereignty as the needs and circumstances required, but generally stopped short of total endorsement of a European union. The maximalists (essentially Christian Democrats) included those dedicated Europeans who placed emphasis first and foremost on the goal of European integration, however obtained and in whatever form. Since no majority could be obtained at the Assembly without some collaboration between at least two of these three groups, the evolution of France's European policy was dictated by the measure of assent which the group in power could extract from its parliamentary partners. So European unification, inasmuch as it depended on France's consent, depended upon the unification of the French political system.[3]

During a first phase (1947–50) and under the direction of the minimalists, the European policy of France was one of co-operation. The principal organizations (OEEC, Council of Europe) were characterized by a simple constitutional framework with an executive organ strictly responsible to governmental authority, an Assembly which was only facultative, and a judiciary which was generally regarded as superfluous.[4]

The emphasis changed from co-operation to integration when the issue of German rearmament convinced the minimalists of the validity of the supranational idea. Integration came to mean reduction of Germany's military potential and restraint of her aggressive instincts. The organizations born, or merely devised, during this period (1950–55) were characterized by their ability to exercise their powers without having to go through the intermediary of national governments. The existence of an Assembly was now desirable as a means of debating policies while a very intricate juridical order, represented by a powerful Court of Justice, became indispensable.

In 1952, this coalition was reduced to its least common denominator when the nationalists (the Gaullists) entered the govern-

---

[3] Mattei Dogan, "France," in *European Assemblies*, ed. Kenneth Lindsay (London, 1960), p. 159.

[4] See, for example, Paul Reuter, *Organisations Européennes* (Paris, 1965).

ment, and when a large fraction of the minimalists began to believe that neither the European Defense Community (EDC) nor the subsequent European Political Community (EPC) were sufficient to guarantee France against the eventuality of a German revival. The idea of European unification seemed to be abandoned until a *relance européenne* could be promoted on a new base of economic growth. The Common Market as a means to achieve further integration was thus the outcome of a stalemate among groups unable to reach a compromise on the political nature of the new Europe being built.

## II

Discussing a policy of which he had been one of the main architects, Robert Schuman explained to the European Assembly that his government was attached "to the idea of European solutions because it is convinced that no other policy is capable of delivering the European countries from their divisions." [5] The first task was less to build Europe than to prevent its further dismemberment. European unity was a mere facet of former wartime Allied unity, to which France was still fundamentally attached. Of course, this unity would be, like the former one, aimed primarily at Germany, as Robert Schuman defined the sole task of this policy to be that of "seeking and finding . . . solutions to the concrete problems which face us in the immediate future." [6] The various schemes offered or accepted by France to meet practical needs would thus vary: the OEEC to respond to economic problems, and the Council of Europe to satisfy the pressure of public opinion. The OEEC might also have served to resume links with Eastern Europe and the Soviet Union, had not the Paris Conference, initiated by Bidault and attended by Bevin and Molotov, disclosed Russia's unwillingness to join in such a form of association with the West.

[5] Council of Europe, Consultative Assembly, *Debates* (Nov. 24, 1950), p. 1688.
[6] *Ibid.*

Evidence, however, shows that at first the French government did not consider the issue of a European organization particularly important.[7] Domestically, it was merely an official gesture of concession toward an elite public which, to some extent, had been stirred by the European idea following the collapse of nationalism during the war and the failure of universalism with the United Nations. Outwardly, it was a reconciliation with the United States' position, as the Congress had made the grant of foreign aid conditional upon "the continuous effort of participating countries to achieve a common program of recovery—and to set up a permanent organization to this end." [8]

Moreover, as subsequent French governments faced the Cold War and found it impossible to place France in the position of intermediary between the two Super Powers, they perceived the advantages of some form of union as a first step toward the creation of a European super state within which France, together with England, would exercise a predominant influence. Such a super state would grow out of a net of economic, social, and military alliances fashioned around a Paris-London axis cemented at Dunkirk. Europe, then, would be united in order to recover prestige which nation states alone could not regain. But still, such a Europe implied the need to contain Germany, and France wanted to see in a European union the same automaticity obtained from Great Britain at Dunkirk.

Fundamentally, there are two concepts of Europe. The first is imperial, a forceful concept based on one center of attraction so powerful that it can establish hegemony *de facto* and *de jure* over most, if not all, of the nations of the Continent. The second is federal, a democratic concept in which European unity is based on an equal division of sovereignty among the associated states. Paradoxically, the supranational idea of Great Britain has traditionally been

[7] Karl Lowenstein, "The Union of Western Europe—Illusion and Reality," *Columbia Law Review*, Vol. 52, No. 1 (January, 1952), pp. 65–66.
[8] Arthur H. Robertson, *The Council of Europe, Its Structure, Functions, and Achievements* (London, 1956), p. 8.

the latter, an idea of federation, while the French were more anxious to realize the idea of empire.[9] After the war, however, several considerations made the British wary of a federalized Europe. First, the special relationship developed between Great Britain and the United States during the war years depended on an independent British diplomacy. Similarly, it was deemed impossible to be both part of the Commonwealth and part of Europe.[10] Second, the Labour party, which headed the government until the fall of 1951, feared close arrangements with non-Socialist countries when the main levers of England's economy were being brought under state control. Finally, as the "European" area could only be confined to the free and democratic states, there was a marked reluctance to enter into any formal European agreement that would signify the division of Europe by excluding the Soviet-controlled states of Eastern Europe as well as the totalitarian states of Southern Europe.[11] Confronted with so many vocations, Great Britain demanded that European unity be promoted step by step by increasing association through traditional treaties.[12]

Early in 1948, Bevin recognized that Britain could not "stand outside Europe and regard her problems as separate from those of her European neighbors." [13] But in the same breath, he also seemed

[9] Altiero Spinelli, "The Growth of the European Movement since World War II" in C. Grove Haines (ed.), *European Integration* (Baltimore, Maryland, 1957), p. 39.

[10] See Bevin's speech of Sept. 15, 1948, *Parliamentary Debates* (Commons), Vol. 456, col. 106ff.

[11] On Feb. 27, 1947, the Labour Cabinet stated its position by rejecting the schemes offered by Churchill and other Europeanists as "more likely to lead to disunity than to unity." Quoted in Frederick Northedge, *British Foreign Policy, the Process of Readjustment, 1945–1961* (London, 1962), p. 47.

[12] Underlying all this was also Great Britain's avowed reluctance to associate with nations on the Continent which "by the attitude of contempt and cynicism which they have adopted toward their own Parliaments, have greatly reduced the prestige and influence and health of parliamentary democratic institutions." Duncan Sandys, Council of Europe, Consultative Assembly (Aug. 28, 1950), *Debates*, p. 1186.

[13] Quoted in Northedge, *British Foreign Policy*, p. 46.

to rule out a common political framework for Western Europe. What he had in mind was a number of bilateral military and defensive pacts with the Western European countries rather than a single political complex. In the field of economic recovery, too, Bevin was emphatic in rejecting a closely knit federation. He insisted instead on a strictly functional form of co-operation, particularly in food production, coal mining, and transport.[14] The Labour government, like the French government, made it a matter of practicality to place itself resolutely in favor of integration within the traditional framework of international law—to deal with practical matters in a practical way—but resolutely against integration involving any abrogation of sovereignty.[15]

Not only a compromise between the French minimalists and the French maximalists, the Council of Europe was also the result of a halfway measure between the French and English governmental views. Simply described, the Council consisted of a ministerial committee meeting in private and a consultative body meeting in public. Obviously, the ministers could obstruct and destroy privately what the delegates debated and solved in public. According to Paul Reynaud, a dedicated Europeanist, the Council of Europe consisted of two bodies—one in favor of European integration, the other against it.[16]

The aim of the Council, set up in August, 1949, was a closer unity between all like-minded countries of Europe.[17] In other words, those countries would participate which would agree to "the principles of the rule of law and of the enjoyment by all persons within its jurisdiction of human rights and fundamental freedom" (Article 3). There was nothing novel in such a concept,

[14] Speech to the Foreign Press Association, June 13, 1947. *Ibid.*, p. 48.

[15] Prime Minister Clement Attlee, *Parliamentary Debates* (Commons), Vol. 450 (May 5, 1948), col. 1318.

[16] *Unite or Perish* (New York, 1951), p. 199.

[17] On the Council, see Robertson, *The Council of Europe*. Also, Frederick L. Schuman, "The Council of Europe," *American Political Science Review*, Vol. XLV, No. 3 (September, 1951), pp. 724–40.

except that it was made an explicit condition of membership (Article 4), and its betrayal could cause exclusion (Article 8). Besides Eastern Europe, the Council was thus closed to Portugal and Spain, two members of the OEEC, which was itself dedicated to the preservation of individual liberty.

Beyond this emphasis on the spiritual and moral character of the European community, the statute stressed economic and social progress through closer unity and association. Contrary to the term union explicitly used in the Resolution adopted by the Hague Congress of Europe in May, 1948, neither unity nor association referred in any way to the federal goal, a union. Here, too, lay indication of a concession to the English viewpoint. At the same time, the emphasis on *closer* association meant—when placed in its context—a dissatisfaction with existing associations, particularly the OEEC. Finally, matters of national defense were left specifically outside the scope of the Council, supposedly because they were to be reserved to NATO.

Among the institutions created by the Council, the Consultative Assembly was different from the usual international organization on at least three counts. First, a system of proportional representation was adopted, with France, Germany, Italy, and Great Britain receiving the highest number. In effect, such a representation gave them an absolute majority at the Assembly (Article 26). Second, the delegates to the Assembly, the status of which was incompatible with that of the Council of Ministers, were to be elected by their respective national parliaments, thus liberating the Assembly, in principle at least, from tight governmental control (Article 25).[18] Third, and as an implication of this latter point, delegates were to originate from all national parties, including those of the opposition, provided they conformed to the already mentioned Article 3. Thus they excluded the national Communist parties from the European Assembly.

The powers of the Assembly were greatly limited. It was com-

[18] This clause was facultative, and representatives of Great Britain remained appointed by their government.

pletely subordinated to the Council of Ministers which represented the various governments concerned. The latter's permission was necessary before any subject could be debated by the Assembly, at least until an amendment adopted at the close of the first session left it free to determine its own agenda within the scope of the statute of the Council of Europe, that is, excepting defense matters (Article 23). Finally, the Assembly could only make recommendations to the Council of Ministers, as no function was deemed limited enough by the Ministers to entrust the Assembly with real powers.

For France, as for Great Britain, the Council of Europe hardly went beyond the Brussels Treaty of the previous year. This agreement had provided, among other things, for the creation of a Consultative Assembly so organized as to be able to exercise its functions continuously with the broad task of holding discussions on all questions related to economic, social, and cultural collaboration and collective self-defense. The newly created Council of Ministers, whose conclusions could only be recommended to the nation members, merely represented a broad enlargement of the Brussels creation. The European Assembly itself was less a gesture of France's good will toward England (or vice versa) than a recognition by both governments of the need to remain continually in touch with European public opinion.[19] Nevertheless, the Council of Europe, which was more than a standing international conference, afforded a constitutional opportunity for an intermediary where the Europeanists could discuss and present their views to the governments on further arrangements of a supranational nature.[20] At the same time, the Council gave a concrete expression to the European idea and stimulated contacts between political parties across national frontiers.[21]

[19] For a text of the Statute, see *Annuaire Européen*, I (The Hague, Holland, 1955), 274–90.

[20] Arnold J. Zurcher, *The Struggle to Unite Europe, 1940–1958* (New York, 1958), p. 46.

[21] Mary M. Ball, *NATO and the European Union Movement* (London. 1959), p. 149.

## III

The failure of France to implement her German policy opened new perspectives toward European unification, which came to be identified with an agreement between those two countries.[22] "It is in the light of the German question that we consider the whole European situation," declared Couve de Murville, who was then Ambassador in Washington, "When we speak of the necessity of building a unified Europe, we imply as a prerequisite the establishment of a Franco-German co-operation."[23] Here, too, the European policy of France moved to meet practical needs: the need to internationalize the Ruhr was satisfied by the European Coal and Steel Community (ECSC), while the EDC was meant to preempt the need for German rearmament. But a contradiction was implicit in the French efforts. While some measure of supranationality was required to entangle Germany sufficiently, the presence of Great Britain was indispensable in order to outweigh Germany within a supranational device limited to Western Europe. Yet, as we have seen, Great Britain was not prepared to enter any such association. Hence the reluctance displayed by France—apparently involved in a little Europe which she did not want—"with two defeated and three tiny countries."[24]

From a Europeanist point of view, the first phase of the policy had been rather frustrating. "The political framework of Western Europe," Hans Schmitt has written, "which had been completely restored in 1945, was in no way modified by the OEEC."[25] Whatever the nature of the post-war restoration of the European frame-

[22] See, for example, Georges Bidault's speech at Hunter College, New York. French Embassy, *Speeches and Press Conferences*, No. 8 (April, 1953).

[23] Address delivered before the Chicago Council of Foreign Relations, *ibid.* (Jan. 10, 1956), No. 54.

[24] General Aumeran, *J.O., Deb., A.N.* (Aug. 29, 1956), p. 4437.

[25] *Path to European Union*, p. 24.

work, it is certain that the OEEC did very little to affect it. Margaret Ball, among others, reaches an identical conclusion.[26] Even from an economic point of view, the union was far from perfect. According to Altiero Spinelli, the OEEC was "one of the greatest deceptions in modern European history" because the money given by the United States to help the Europeans overcome economic nationalism "served only to reconstitute the old national economies, instead of creating one market and one European economy." [27] Charges made by some at the Council of Europe reflected frustrations felt by many Europeanists. "What exactly has OEEC done?" asked Paul Reynaud. "On the question of unblocking of trade channels, we have not yet gone back to the period preceding the 1929 crisis. In fact—Reynaud continued—it has endeavored by every means at its disposal to obstruct our action." [28] Obstructed on one side by the OEEC and on the other by the Council of Ministers, the Council of Europe had become—Reynaud concluded—"a mutual admiration society" [29]—about which other analysts found it hard not to be sarcastic.[30]

In European circles, therefore, there developed an awareness that a desire to preserve unanimity made it necessary to keep step with the state most hesitant, not to say most hostile, regarding any structural reform. "Since the end of the war," wrote Maurice Duverger early in 1950, "the whole history of Europe is the story of the concessions made to England. All European organizations have been emptied of any substance so that Great Britain could join them." [31] This feeling of dissatisfaction was embraced by the French government, where minimalist and maximalist Europeanists agreed to refuse further concessions or compromises, particu-

[26] Mary M. Ball, *NATO and the European Union*, pp. 217ff.

[27] See Haines, *European Integration*, p. 54.

[28] Council of Europe, Consultative Assembly. *Debates* (Aug. 9, 1950), p. 64. Reynaud was making allusion to the necessity for the Assembly "to have regard to the work of other European intragovernmental organizations." (Article 23, par. b).

[29] *Ibid.*, p. 65.

[30] Georg Schwarzenberger, *Power Politics* (2d ed.; New York, 1951), p. 785.

[31] Quoted in *L'Année Politique, 1950,* p. 140.

larly as Europe was now seen as a means of containing Germany. "We cannot subordinate the creation of Europe to the approval of one single European country," said Georges Bidault, who also pleaded that "the credit account opened by geography for the history of Great Britain is now exhausted."[32] Yet, there could be no talk of federation before considering the foundations on which it could be reared without Britain.[33] The European Coal and Steel Community, the European Defense Community, and the European Political Community were the three schemes devised by the maximalists to rally the minimalists to a new supranational Europe. The absence of Great Britain would be compensated for by a more traditional form of alliance with her alone.

Actually, the French government made it more difficult for Great Britain to accept the ECSC by offering the treaty without prior notice and by asking her, like the other interested parties, to subscribe beforehand to a public statement of agreement with the principles contained in Schuman's declaration of May 9, 1950, more particularly with the principle of supranationality.[34] For the French, the importance of supranational authority stemmed from their desire to control Germany. Robert Schuman would readily admit, a few years later, that the High Authority was seen as a device "to enable Germany to accept restrictions on her own sovereignty, which was being gradually restored to her."[35] Since this was the main aim of the French proposal, it is easy to understand why they chose to maintain their principle of the High Authority in relation to Germany, rather than see Great Britain take part in the negotiations. They feared that the presence of Great Britain in the negotiations would, once more, adulterate the central idea of the Schuman Plan. And as a matter of fact, the counter proposal

[32] Council of Europe, Consultative Assembly, *Debates* (Nov. 23, 1950), p. 1588.

[33] *Ibid.*, p. 1586.

[34] On supranationality, see Ernst B. Haas, *The Uniting of Europe* (Stanford, 1958), pp. 32ff.

[35] Quoted in Roy F. Willis, *France, Germany, and the New Europe*, p. 104.

offered later by Great Britain at the Council of Europe called for an international authority whose member countries, endowed with the number of votes in proportion to their coal and steel production, would still be left with the right to veto or to withdraw.[36]

If the Community was political in origin, it was more so in its objective. At the conclusion of the debates on the Petersberg Agreements of November, 1949, the National Assembly had demanded in its final resolution an internationalization of the Ruhr, both as a means to achieve security and as the indispensable preliminary to the creation of a united Europe.[37] In the thirties an industrial revolution, based on newly developed chemical and improved metallurgical processes, had given coal utmost importance as a raw material and as the foundation of industrial production.[38] Hence, Schuman made his bold assertion that the placing of the entire Franco-German production of coal and steel under a common High Authority would make any war between France and Germany materially impossible.

The proposal contained potentialities which, in the estimation of the French government, could rapidly lead toward the complete economic and political unification of Europe.[39] The Schuman Plan marked the endorsement by its sponsor of the functional thesis. European unification would be accomplished first in the economic realm. But at the same time, it was expected that political unification would arise out of the fusion of interests thus created among European nations.[40]

From an economic standpoint, however, the performance of the Community was hampered precisely by its functional restrictions.

[36] Anthony Nutting, *Europe Will Not Wait: A Warning and a Way Out* (London, 1960), p. 42.

[37] Quoted in Willis, *France, Germany, and the New Europe*, p. 69.

[38] See Frederick Sethur, "The Schuman Plan and Ruhr Coal," *Political Science Quarterly*, Vol. LXVII, No. 4 (December, 1952).

[39] Robert Schuman, Council of Europe, Consultative Assembly, *Debates* (Aug. 10, 1950), p. 99.

[40] See R. Schuman's foreword to Paul Reuter, *La Communauté Européenne du Charbon et de l'Acier* (Paris, 1953), p. 4.

Not only was it pledged to attain the most rational distribution of production at the highest level of productivity (Article 2) in the field of coal and steel, but it was also pledged, in a more general vein, to the over-all objectives of promoting economic growth, furthering full employment, and improving standards of living in the participating states. Yet restricted as it was, the Community could hardly interfere with such things as monetary and fiscal problems, taxes, wages, and social security—all of crucial importance to the stated economic objectives. It was no wonder that the difficulties in the realization of the Schuman Plan began where economic problems left off.[41] But, again, these problems were expected to be solved rapidly through a further extension of the integrating process. The Community was not regarded as an isolated institution but as the pilot for a new form of supranational co-operation, only one side of a triangle in which the other two were the Defense and the Political communities.

The European Political Community was linked to both the community which sponsored it and the ill-fated EDC which required it. This double origin explains its particular interest: the EPC was drafted by hard-nosed politicians who acted at the formal request of the governments concerned. At first, the French government supported it to defeat the opposition of the Socialists and the Gaullists to the defense treaty. We must recall that the latter had described Europe as "a fiction." As to the Socialists, their insistence on a supranational political authority was but one of their numerous preliminaries.[42] But these governmental efforts were to be of no avail, as the EPC itself remained unacceptable to both parties. Even though the draft offered to the newly formed Assembly of the Community was unanimously accepted (50–0), the French Socialists accounted for three of the five abstentions—the other two were credited to the German Socialists on grounds that Great Britain would not join such a scheme. As to the three Gaullists,

[41] William Diebold, Jr., *The Schuman Plan* (New York, 1959), p. 66.
[42] See Guy Mollet, Council of Europe, Consultative Assembly, *Debates* (May 29, 1952), pp. 207–10.

they did not vote at all. The fact of the matter is that by 1953–54, the urgency which existed in 1949–50 and which had prompted the minimalists to participate in a European majority had faded away, thereby enabling those same minimalists to return to their former opposition.


IV


Actually, there was no European majority among French political parties at any time during the whole of the Fourth Republic. The passage of the ECSC had been due to an *ad hoc* alliance between minimalists and maximalists, with Germany acting as a common denominator. The agreement over the EDC and the EPC was temporary, and the Alliance, as we have seen earlier, split when half of the minimalists joined the Communists and nationalists in their opposition to those schemes.

The foundations of a *relance européenne* were laid at the Messina conference in June, 1955. But the agreement reached there was only on principles, the contents of which were left dependent upon further study. Moreover, the French government accepted the Messina Agreement on condition that the committee which it set up under the leadership of Paul-Henry Spaak could not draft treaties but must confine itself to the study of methods.[43]

The political situation in France was not basically changed after the elections of January, 1956.[44] The great defeat of the Gaullists did not mean an improvement of the position of the Europeanists, as it was largely compensated for by gains of the Communists and extreme Right. In 1951, Communists and Gaullists had accounted for 224 votes at the Assembly. Of these, 217 voted against the ECSC and 182 against the EDC (the majority of the extreme right voted in favor of both). After the 1956 elections, Commu-

[43] Jean-François Poncet, quoted in Willis, *France, Germany, and the New Europe*, p. 244.

[44] Haas, *Uniting of Europe*, p. 127. Europe played an unimportant role during the campaign.

nists and Gaullists, who now accounted for 172 deputies, were joined by 52 Poujadists in their opposition to European integration, for a similar total of 224 deputies. In January, 1957, most of these deputies opposed the government on the project of a Common Market, while in July of the same year their position toward the proposed Rome Treaty largely reflected the same stubborn opposition.

Nevertheless, the defeat of the Gaullists meant that no meaningful opposition to European integration would now exist within the government as it could be taken for granted that neither the Communists nor the Poujadists would participate in any governmental coalition. This was all the more true after Mendès-France split with Guy Mollet and the *Front Républicain*. Mendès-France, who described himself as always having been "in favor of an economic construction of Europe," thought that the re-establishment of French political order and the rejuvenation of the French economy must precede the building of Europe.[45] Within the government, as within the French Assembly, the minimalists of the SFIO clearly held the balancing position. This was true despite the change of heart of the non-Gaullist right whose pro-integration majority had largely increased as a result of their satisfaction with the Coal and Steel Community.[46]

As in 1950–52, the alliance between minimalists and maximalists was largely due to international events. More than any other democratic government, the French government showed a tendency to wait for external constraint before acting, because of its domestic instability. Only then could the unmovable forces of the opposition find a common ground of understanding. "World events," remarked Maurice Faure, who was at that time in charge of European affairs, "have influenced and accelerated the nature of the negotiation." [47] In this case, the Suez crisis was the catalyst. Coming between Indochina and Algeria, it highlighted the inability of the Atlantic Alliance to protect interests which France might deem

[45] *J.O., Deb., A.N.* (Jan. 17, 1957), p. 159.
[46] Haas, *Uniting of Europe*, p. 121.
[47] *J.O., Deb., A.N.* (Jan. 16, 1957), p. 70.

vital. The Atlantic Alliance could only be effective in a situation where the interests of the United States coincided with those of her European partners. But obviously these interests could not always be identical. The Atlantic Alliance arose out of a European crisis of confidence; an Atlantic crisis of confidence now promoted European unification. The construction of a united Europe was more urgent and necessary, since the only option left to France was the uncertain future of her isolation.[48] Thus, it was not the view of the maximalists which prevailed, a view according to which "if we do not make Europe, others will do it without us." [49] Once more, the French government was making it a matter of practicality, since if left alone, France would be subjected to an endless procession of "threats by Mr. Bulganin, humiliation by the United Nations, . . . ridicule by Cairo . . . and misunderstanding from her best friends." [50]

The minimalists were now more agreeable to the idea of a "little Europe" which—they thought—could emerge with the sort of Anglo-French special relationship seemingly forged during the Suez crisis. "The agreement which we have just achieved between our two countries is a political fact which is extremely important for the future development of European . . . politics," Premier Guy Mollet had announced at the National Assembly.[51] In another instance, he suggested that "the *Entente Cordiale* has never been as much alive as now." [52]

Furthermore, the Socialists saw in this little Europe "the embryo, the seed of a Europe of Sixteen or Seventeen," and they were convinced that Great Britain would ultimately join with the remaining European nations.[53] The maximalists fully agreed, as they also foresaw an association of the Common Market with "other

[48] Christian Pineau, Foreign Minister, *ibid.* (Jan. 22, 1957), p. 203.
[49] Paul Reynaud, *ibid.*
[50] P. H. Teitgen, *ibid.* (Jan. 15, 1957), p. 10.
[51] *Ibid.* (Nov. 7, 1956).
[52] A statement made during Queen Elizabeth's visit to Paris, quoted in *L'Année Politique, 1957*, p. 333.
[53] Gilles Gozard, *J.O., Deb., A.N.* (Jan. 16, 1957), p. 79. See also Guy Mollet, *ibid.*, p. 216, and P. O. Lapie, *ibid.*, p. 107.

European countries within the larger framework of a free trade area." [54]

The opposition tried vainly to revive the former reservations of the SFIO. Pierre Cot, as always the most articulate of the Communists and their affiliates, suggested that the French government wanted "to marry Germany but, once in a while, go and have a cup of tea with Great Britain." [55] Mendès-France went one step further and argued that Great Britain had been kept deliberately out of the new organization and that her future entry had been largely compromised by a refusal to let her participate in the negotiations as observers.[56]

But, as Foreign Minister Christian Pineau pointed out, there could be no choice between a small Common Market and a large free trade area, as Great Britain showed an interest in the latter only so far as the former was instituted.[57] Furthermore, such a trade area would exclude the colonies and agriculture, both primary concerns of the Assembly. Finally, there was a definite consensus in the Assembly that the association of Great Britain with Europe should not be obtained at the cost of those maximum guarantees which had been painfully extracted by the French government from its five European partners.

Within such a context, Germany was the forgotten factor of the *relance européenne*. The aggressiveness of the extreme left was still fettered by the remnants of the détente which the Soviets had tried to institute until the Hungarian crisis, while for those of the extreme right the place given to agriculture was the most impor tant source of concern.[58] Suez had shown that an Anglo-French alliance did not carry enough power, so it was necessary to supplement it with a European alliance, and West Germany naturally had to be a part of it. The measures of security provided by the

[54] Maurice Faure, *ibid.* (Jan. 16, 1957), p. 76.

[55] *Ibid.* (Jan. 22, 1957), p. 198.

[56] *Ibid.*, p. 197. Foreign Minister Pineau denied those charges (*ibid.*). Mendès-France's charges had also been expressed by *The Economist* of Jan. 19, 1957.

[57] *J.O., Deb., A.N., ibid.*

[58] See, for example, Dorgères' statement, *ibid.* (Jan. 15, 1957), pp. 7–8.

Paris Agreements of 1954 were thus deemed sufficient. Only the possible reunification of both Germanys and its consequences upon the projected treaty still aroused concern.[59] At any rate, the government was aware that "inasmuch as the economy of the greater part of Germany will be oriented toward Western Europe, the attraction of the West will be felt considerably by a reunified Germany." [60]

The European policy of France is often acclaimed as the cornerstone of the foreign policy of the Fourth Republic.[61] But its development was mostly accidental. Of the three ideologies—*relance nationale*, European unity, and Atlantic community—upon which French governments hesitated, it is the last that was chosen first. Even divided, Europe could still survive so long as its constituent states remained integrated in an Atlantic community under the protection of the United States. The European idea was used to patch up the Atlantic differences. The ECSC and the EDC were compromises between the United States' and the French positions over policy with regard to Germany's heavy industry and rearmament. But the Suez venture revealed that there were cases when differences of interest could not always be settled in a manner satisfactory to all concerned. The growth of European unity thus resulted from a decline in Atlantic unity.

The *relance européenne* itself made possible a *relance nationale*. By agreeing to harmonize economic burdens and by consenting to share certain colonial costs, the partners in the Common Market greatly helped the French economy in its revival.

EURATOM provided a most vivid illustration of the connection between the *relance européenne* and the *relance nationale*.[62] It was devoid of authority to prevent any member country from going ahead with a nuclear military program.[63] This was contrary

[59] Pierre André, *ibid.*, p. 14.

[60] Christian Pineau, *ibid.* (Jan. 18, 1957), p. 158.

[61] Grosser, *La IVème République et sa Politique Extérieure*, p. 403.

[62] On EURATOM, see Lawrence Scheinman, *Atomic Energy Policy in France under the Fourth Republic* (Princeton, N.J., 1965).

[63] Ben Moore, quoted in Alvin J. Cottrell and James E. Dougherty, *The Politics of the Atlantic Alliance* (New York, 1964), p. 133.

to the original expectations of the Europeanists, who had hoped that the treaty would forbid nuclear military activities by any member without approval of at least half of them.[64] But the French consensus on this point was clear: "As to the question of whether or not France must have an atomic armament, the members of the Commission on National Defense all agree, with the exception of the Communists." [65] The European vocation of France was indeed so uncertain that even the Gaullists, who voted in favor of EURATOM, could consent to much of it. At any rate, the future of the treaties was also uncertain, since the Gaullists were announcing that their return to power would imply the renunciation of all European commitments.[66]

[64] Leonard Beaton and John Maddox, *The Spread of Nuclear Weapons* (New York, 1962), p. 84.

[65] Pierre André, Rapporteur, *J.O., Deb., A.N.* (July 3, 1957), p. 3187.

[66] After Michel Debré's diatribe against the Treaties of Rome, de Gaulle is supposed to have commented: "What for? After returning to power, we will tear up these treaties." Quoted in Paul Reynaud, *The Foreign Policy of Charles de Gaulle* (New York, 1964), p. 51.

✤ ✤ ✤ ✤

# CHAPTER FOUR

# THE CONDITIONS OF DECLINE

✤ ✤ ✤ ✤ ✤

## I

At the structural level, the parliamentary system of the Fourth Republic was characterized by ministerial instability combined with a pronounced weakness of the executive. This combination inevitably produced incoherent government by the legislature. Government by the National Assembly in turn led to the problem of decision-making, as the legislature remained unable to reach lasting agreement on major issues.

The responsibility for governmental instability should not be attributed simply to the multiplicity and diversity of the political parties. In effect, the multiparty system of France merely reflects the spontaneous expression of the major political attitudes— from right to left, Conservative, Liberal (and, in a predominantly Catholic society, Christian Democrat), and Socialist. In addition, both ends of the French political spectrum have traditionally been open to extreme tendencies—broadly speaking, the authoritative on the extreme right, and the Communist on the extreme left.[1]

This basic division, however, was blurred by fluidity along most ideological lines. For Guy Mollet, for instance, the Socialist party was "essentially national."[2] All parties would obviously make the same claim, while none could ever further explain the actual con-

[1] Raymond Aron, *France, Steadfast and Changing* (Cambridge, 1960), p. 79.

[2] Quoted in Alfred Grosser, *La IVème République et sa Politique Extérieure*, p. 118.

71

tent of the national essence. The Mouvement Républicain Populaire (MRP), founded in 1944 to spread Christian democratic consciousness, could nevertheless be called neither in its title nor in its vocation a Catholic party.[3] By its first president, Maurice Schumann, it was described as essentially "the party of fidelity." [4] At that time, Schumann thought primarily in terms of fidelity to General de Gaulle. Later, Robert Schuman would shift the direction of the ascribed fidelity toward the idea of European unity. In either case, the MRP was, in the words of Guy Mollet, "a party that should not exist." [5] Such lack of doctrine in turn facilitated the division of these parties into factions emerging according to developing power struggles between incompatible personalities. Through the years, for instance, the Radical party had become "a gathering of well-bred people who . . . do their best not to agree on anything," [6] and Jacques Soustelle, then a fervent Gaullist, took pleasure in describing it as "not a group of thirty deputies, but thirty groups of one deputy." [7] In his history of the Fourth Republic, Jacques Barsalou has described, as determining for the various governments concerned, the personal altercations which at one time or another pitted de Gaulle against Georges Bidault, Guy Mollet *vs.* Paul Ramadier, Joseph Daniel *vs.* Roger Duchet, and René Mayer *vs.* Pierre Mendès-France, as well as opposing Jules Moch to the Communists, P. H. Teitgen to the Radicals, and Antoine Pinay to the Gaullists.[8]

More important, however, is the fact that side by side with these political and personal differences grew more crucial antagonisms concerning three issues which kept cropping up simultaneously: the struggle between democracy and authoritarian government,

[3] Jacques Fauvet, *La France Déchirée* (Paris, 1957), p. 59.

[4] Quoted in André Geraud, "France Gets to Her Feet," *Foreign Affairs*, Vol. XXVII, No. 3 (April, 1949), p. 396.

[5] Quoted in Pierre Fougeyrollas, *La Conscience Politique dans la France Contemporaine* (Paris, 1963), p. 93.

[6] Jacques Fauvet, *La France Déchirée*, p. 23.

[7] *Paris Match*, Jan. 3–9, 1953. Quoted by Nathan Leites, *Images of Power in French Politics*, RAND Memorandum, RM/2954/RC (June, 1962), I, 133.

[8] *La Mal Aimée, passim.*

between employer and employee, and between nationalism and Catholicism. Inability to agree on the constitutional problem pitted Conservatives and Gaullists against the left, for the right has traditionally sought a strong executive whereas the left has fought for a strong legislative.[9] Roy Macridis put it very aptly: "According to the Right, the State embodies the legitimate interests of the people; while according to the Left, these interests are identified only with the people." [10] So efforts to undertake badly needed constitutional changes would usually engender the fall of the existing governmental majority and a realignment of political forces.

In the economic realm, the Socialists and a large fraction of the MRP (and, of course, the Communists) did not accept the liberal economic policy advocated by part of the Radicals and by the Conservatives, since that policy was more solicitous of the interests of management than of wage earners. On the other hand, the right and some of the Radicals were still disinclined to make concessions to any Socialist *dirigisme*, despite the success of the first Monnet Plan which directed the postwar resurgence of the French economy. Paralleling these disputes ran the controversy over *écoles libres* vs. *écoles laïques*. The MRP resolved to persist in its effort to secure financial help for the private schools, all the more so in the late forties and early fifties when the Gaullists were trying to regain the MRP's Catholic voters by claiming that the MRP was ready to sacrifice the private schools to their political alliance with the Socialists. The MRP and its allies from the right were thus engaged in a stubborn conflict with the left, dedicated as it was to the "lay laws" of 1886, denying any aid coming from public funds, whether those of the central government, the provinces, or the towns, to the private (religious) primary schools.

[9] The following are the meanings of the main terms used in the *Journal Officiel*: Extreme right: *Républicains Sociaux*; Right: *Modérés*; Center: MRP; Left: Radicals and Socialists (SFIO); Extreme left: Communists (PC).

[10] Roy Macridis and Bernard Brown, *The de Gaulle Republic* (Homewood, Ill., 1960), p. 120. According to de Gaulle, "the Left is against the state, and the Right is against the nation." Quoted in Georgette Elgey, *La République des Illusions*, p. 193.

With these questions always looming in the background, it was difficult for any government to obtain a majority, or once this majority had been obtained, to preserve it. The religious quarrel prevented any lasting coalition between the non-Communist left and the MRP. The institutional quarrel would prevent Socialists and Conservatives from eventually acting together. The economic differences would oppose the left, this time allied with the MRP, to the right. In 1951, for instance, there was a rapid succession of governments which, temporarily, drew the executive out of its apathy by providing one majority for each problem, one government for each solution.[11] So, the Queuille government secured a majority constituted of the Moderates, the Radicals, the Socialists, and the MRP to set up the forthcoming elections. It was succeeded by the Pleven government, which disposed of the religious problem by uniting Gaullists, Moderates, and the MRP. René Pleven was then replaced by Edgar Faure, who concentrated on economic and social measures by uniting the Socialists and the Radicals with the MRP.

The following table, often quoted, will help to convey the general attitude of the main political groups in these three essential domestic fields:

| Education | Communist | Socialist | Radical | Christian Democrats | Right | Gaullist |
|---|---|---|---|---|---|---|
| State monopoly | X | X | | | | |
| Neither monopoly nor subsidy for religious schools | | | X | | | |
| Subsidy | | | | X | X | X |
| *Economic Policy* | | | | | | |
| Collectivist | X | | | | | |
| *Dirigiste* | | X | | X | | |
| Liberal | | | X | | X | X |
| *Political structure* | | | | | | |
| People's democracy | X | | | | | |
| Parliamentary democracy | | X | X | X | X | |
| "Authoritarian" democracy | | | | | | X |

[11] Fauvet, *La France Déchirée*, p. 103.

After the elections of 1956, the constitution of a majority became still more arduous with the presence, at both political extremes of the "hexagonal Chamber," of 35 per cent of the deputies irreversibly opposed to any measure proposed by the government.[12] Given such a party distribution, the moderate left could not govern with the extreme left since it would appear revolutionary, but it could not govern without it either, since it did not have sufficient votes to go it alone in the Assembly. Similarly, the Conservatives could neither govern with the extreme right, nor without it: in the former case, they would be reactionary; in the latter, they would be in the minority.[13] The only solution was for the moderate left to form a coalition, temporarily, with the moderate right. The government, be it of the right or left, would survive as long as it followed the policy of its counterpart—for the time being its ally. Hence the baffling contradiction: a government of the left would support and intensify the war in Algeria, while a government of the right would pass new social laws. Mollet's remark about the French right being "the most imbecile in the world" was equally valid for any single group, as the Assembly had become "a vicious circle which revolves around itself, above and almost independently of the rest of the country." [14]

## II

The influence of such a political *va et vient* was, nevertheless, seemingly minimal in the realm of diplomacy. Writing just before World War II, Arnold Wolfers had noticed that "in no country has the government changed more frequently nor the pendulum

[12] The "hexagonal chamber" included the Communists (25.1 per cent), the Socialists (15.9 per cent), the Radicals and apparented groups (15.3 per cent), the MRP (14.1 per cent), the Conservatives (19.6 per cent), and the extreme right (Poujadists and others: 10 per cent). It was thus impossible for the right or for the left to form a majority independent of the other.

[13] Fauvet, *La France Déchirée*, p. 81.

[14] Stanley Hoffmann, "Politique d'abord," *Esprit* (December, 1957), p. 817.

of political power swung back and forth between groups of parties in such a quick succession." Yet, he continued, "there may be found, under the surface, a surprising degree of unity in matters of foreign policy." [15] Still farther back, the famed historian G. P. Gooch (quoting Albert Sorel as his precursor) had made a similar observation: "In no country of modern Europe have the changes in regime been more frequent, yet nowhere have such revolutionary transformations exercised less influence on the governing principles of diplomacy." [16]

Undoubtedly, French political parties have traditionally expressed little concern for foreign affairs. Actually, throughout the entire period of the Third Republic, there was, so to speak, a foreign policy of the left and one of the right—one promoting international co-operation, peaceful competition, and disarmament, and the other advocating military preparedness, power politics, and national interest[17]—distinctions schematized as *"la méthode de la contrainte"* vs. *"la méthode de la persuasion."* [18] But beyond such verbal distinction all that can be said is that there were between the major political parties (with the exclusion of the Communists) differences in form and temper, rather than in content and direction of the conduct of diplomacy under the Third as well as under the Fourth Republic.

On the whole, the Socialist party was pro-European and pro-American. It played a leading role in the governments which accepted the Marshall Plan, the North Atlantic Alliance, the creation of the West German state and of the Council of Europe. It advocated a foreign policy "based on the independence of the European Community within the Atlantic solidarity," [19] even though when

[15] *Britain and France*, p. 29.

[16] *Before the War. Studies in Diplomacy* (London, 1936), p. 89.

[17] Frederick L. Schuman, *War and Diplomacy in the French Republic* (New York and London, 1931), p. 371. See also Wolfers, *Britain and France*, pp. 29–33.

[18] Raymond Poincaré, *Deb. Sénat* (July 10, 1924), p. 1029. Quoted in Wolfers, *ibid.*, p. 30.

[19] Socialist Congress, Resolution, May 15, 1951. Quoted in *L'Année Politique, 1951*, p. 144.

those various policies had to be implemented the SFIO found itself in the paradoxical situation of being relegated (with the Communists) to the opposition, a situation somewhat similar to that of the Labour Party in England. As seen by the Socialists, Europe was to be built through reconciliation with Germany and close co-operation with Great Britain, particularly during the era of Clement Attlee's Labour government. On this last issue, Guy Mollet and his followers thought that by staying away from Europe, Great Britain would carry with her the Netherlands, which would in turn cause the absence of the other two Benelux countries, leaving France shut up in a "small, dark box" with Italy and Germany.[20] To avoid a development of this type, they called for the creation of a Europe within the framework of the Council of Europe so that all states might enter into the debate even if some had to make reservations and decline to adhere for the time being.[21]

The MRP, the European party *par excellence*, had taken advantage of the discredit cast upon the Radicals, who were too closely associated with the Third Republic, and upon the old right, too closely connected with the Vichy regime. In the words of Jacques Fauvet, the MRP's major problem consisted in "being by birth a governmental party even before being a party at all." [22] Even though more Germany-conscious, its foreign policy was very close to that of the Socialists, on the whole pro-European and pro-American. In fact, as the Socialists were held prisoners of the MRP because of their fear of Gaullism, the MRP's were held prisoners of the Socialists because of their fears of Communism. But unlike the SFIO the MRP, who colonized the Quai d'Orsay, remained in a position to make policy throughout most of the Fourth Republic.

Within the MRP, Georges Bidault was perhaps less European and more nationalist (hence less American) than Robert Schuman. His lesser infatuation with the European idea referred to the tim-

[20] André Philip, *Le Socialisme et l'Unité Européenne* (Paris, 1951), *passim*.

[21] Guy Mollet, Council of Europe, Consultative Assembly, *Debates* (Aug. 28, 1950), p. 1178.

[22] *La France Déchirée*, p. 60.

ing rather than to the principle as such, as he did "not consider internal political conditions . . . at least in some countries, including [France] . . . as permitting the setting up of any particular group." [23] Before their Socialist partners, however, both Bidault and Schuman accepted reduction of the choice to one between a Europe without Great Britain or no Europe at all. As Schuman realized that Great Britain would "at best give European integration her kind blessing, never her complete adherence," [24] Bidault warned that he "personally refused to allow either a Party or a people to prevent endlessly a general [European] build up." [25]

The Gaullists, on the other hand, were opposed to pro-Americanism and pro-Europeanism, inasmuch as they tended to affect French nationalism. Dedicated to the vision of a Europe which, under the leadership of France, would hold the balance of power between East and West, the Gaullists rejected almost every important step taken by the successive governments of the Fourth Republic, including the Marshall Plan, the Atlantic Alliance, the Coal and Steel Community and the Treaty of Rome. Particularly alien to their thinking was the concept of supranationality which they often defined as "the right of decision being surrendered to authorities composed of technicians who are, in practice, responsible to no one." [26] A *rapprochement* with Germany was at first deemed possible only after her dismemberment into a federation of states. But after the advent of the Federal Republic, the Gaullists overlooked, as de Gaulle put it in his speech of September 25, 1949, "the sadness and the anger which are produced . . . among the French people by the very mention of Germany," and concluded that "the unity of Europe must, if possible and despite everything, incorporate the Germans." [27]

[23] Council of Europe, Consultative Assembly, *Debates* (Aug. 28, 1950), p. 1208.

[24] *Ibid.*

[25] Harvard University speech, Ch. 1, note 56.

[26] Michel Debré, Council of Europe, Consultative Assembly, *Debates* (Sept. 17, 1954), p. 447.

[27] Quoted in Roger Massip, *De Gaulle et l'Europe* (Paris, 1963), p. 52.

In the realm of diplomacy, then, a majority was always attainable—usually including the Socialists, the Radicals, the MRP, and the Moderates—so that what most hampered the Fourth Republic was less the clash of opposing political ideologies than the manner in which the government and the Assembly handled the issues of foreign policy. Here too, the Fourth Republic behaved like the Third Republic, as "a machine so well provided with brakes and safety valves that it comes slowly to a state of immobility." [28] For where could any authority be found, and consequently, where could any responsibility be placed? It could not be found in the President of the Republic, whose constitutional task was only to sign and ratify the treaties. He was not to negotiate them—merely "to be kept informed" of the negotiations, as opposed to his function under the Third Republic. Responsibility was not placed either in the Foreign Minister, who was virtually a captive of his government, which was in turn a captive of its majority. Shortly after having been replaced by Georges Bidault, Robert Schuman complained that—as Foreign Minister—he had only limited authority over the men who represented him. Furthermore, he went on, "The minister is not alone in determining the policy to be followed; it is the business of the government . . . within which his opinion . . . does not necessarily prevail. He can, of course, offer his resignation if his personal views are dismissed." But, Schuman concluded, such a course of action would lead to a political crisis, the responsibility for which he was generally unwilling to assume.[29] Any responsibility was equally denied by the ministers who were captive of their parties, as until Pierre Mendès-France it was customary for a Prime Minister to distribute the ministries to the political parties which would in turn hand them over to whomever they might choose. Finally, the Quai d'Orsay discharged itself of any responsibility by claiming that it was too

[28] Mattei Brogan, Introduction to Alexander Werth, *The Twilight of France, 1933–1940* (New York, 1941), p. vi.
[29] Quoted in Grosser, *La IVème République et sa Politique Extérieure,* p. 52.

often bypassed through the functional disintegration of the Ministry. Side by side with the foreign minister, there were, at times, a minister in charge of North African affairs, one in charge of European institutions, or one in charge of the relations with NATO.[30]

Nevertheless, there could still be a policy well defined and well implemented in a system of coalition government, provided that the Assembly be left outside the field of foreign relations and that ministerial solidarity overcome the solidarity of the parties. However, such was not the case. All in all, the National Assembly did not express much interest in foreign affairs. In fact, these concerned, in the larger sense (that is, including the votes on military budget), hardly more than 5 per cent of its debates,[31] and only one-fifth of the votes of confidence taken during the Fourth Republic.[32] It is also true that ministerial instability only slightly affected the direction of the Foreign Ministry, occupied by no more than five men during the whole existence of the Fourth Republic. Nevertheless, Alfred Coste-Floret, among many others, would still claim that "it is here, at the National Assembly, that we must devise the foreign policy of France . . . Any change . . . could only result from a change of majority." [33] Yet, the National Assembly, mostly "called upon to discuss principles, intentions . . . and no precise text" [34] could obviously not devise a foreign policy, but could act merely as a brake to delay its implementation and eventually erode it through endless "preliminary conditions that amounted to disguised refusals." [35] Approved by the parties at the level of broad generalities, an idea would be subjected to increasing criticism as soon as it would run up against the numerous details guiding its application. "One does not proceed by major choices," noticed the then Premier Félix Gaillard, "but by small settlements which have to be made every day." [36]

[30] *Ibid.*, p. 62ff.
[31] Freymond, *The Saar Conflict*, pp. 275–76.
[32] Grosser, *La IVème République et sa Politique Extérieure*, p. 81.
[33] Quoted in *ibid.*, p. 79.
[34] Pierre André, *J.O., Deb., A.N.* (Jan. 15, 1957), p. 14.
[35] Guy Mollet, quoted in Leites, *Images of Power*, I, 65.
[36] Félix Gaillard, *J.O., Deb., A.N.* (Nov. 5, 1957), p. 4652.

By 1957, about one-third of the deputies at the National Assembly (excluding the Communists and the Poujadists) were or had been ministers, thanks to a rotation system which enabled them to enter or to leave a government according to its needs for a parliamentary majority. A reshuffling of a Cabinet would usually be accompanied by a reshuffling of its majority, the extent and frequency of which can be ascertained from a Prime Minister's candid remark (Edgar Faure) that only thirteen deputies never voted for the government which he headed. Such an elasticity would have been made impossible by a rigidity in the governmental doctrine or policy. "The art of politics," as seen by an influential leader of the MRP (P. H. Teitgen) was "not so much a matter of separating 'mine' from 'yours' as of distinguishing 'ours.'"[37] In other words, the task of a government consisted mainly in reaching compromises referring to the correct expedient, rather than to the proper content of the policy covered in an effort to reconcile the directives of the Assembly with the main lines of a policy which, as we have seen, was more France's than any one party's or government's.

But under the Fourth Republic, this struggle for survival became an end in itself, as it became more and more frequently said that the main goal of any government was to stay in power. "French politics," complained François Mauriac, "depend on the necessity of securing the few votes which the President of the Council needs in order to survive."[38] Writing several weeks before the fall of the Mollet government, a noted commentator also reported the increasing rumor in governmental circles that "the main thing is to hold on until the first week in July and that the closing of the session of Parliament will then put off the difficulties until the reopening of Parliament in October."[39] Still more notorious were the efforts of Joseph Laniel, whose main ambition as a Prime Minister was to surpass the record for governmental

[37] *J.O., Deb., A.N.* (Sept. 30, 1957), p. 444.
[38] *Bloc Notes, 1952–1957* (Paris, 1958), p. 15.
[39] Georges Rovtand, *Bulletin du Centre d'Etudes Politiques*, May 7, 1957. Quoted in Leites, *Images of Power*, I, 72.

longevity held by a party fellow with whom he was on rather bad
terms (Antoine Pinay). Laniel, who would actually be asked at
the Assembly "to give the country the feeling that . . . you
[Laniel] are governing it rather than merely trying to hold out
longer than anyone else," [40] had been able to hold on thanks to the
Bermuda conference during the summer of 1953, and the winter
and spring of 1954, to the Berlin and Geneva conferences respectively.

It was thus inescapable that a government engaged in constant
negotiations for survival should seek the best domestic and foreign
tactics to avoid being toppled, thereby making international relations but one more aspect contingent upon domestic politics.

For example, when the National Assembly was to vote on the
Paris Agreements establishing the Western European Union, a
majority of deputies felt that the treaty ought to be ratified in
order to soften the blow to French prestige inflicted by the rejection of the EDC. But a majority of deputies also predicted that it
would be easily ratified. Hence the treaty was first rejected, as
numerous deputies believed that they could abstain or vote against
it without modifying the predicted result, every group and every
individual counting on others to take upon themselves the political
onus of rearming Germany. "I admit that I miscalculated," said
Maurice Schumann, later, explaining his negative vote.[41]

Still more striking was the reversal of the position of the Socialist party whose partial opposition to the EDC was transformed
into a full support for the WEU, even though according to its
sponsor, the differences between both schemes were militarily in-
significant.[42] The fact of the matter is that from the Pinay government (March–December, 1952) to that of Laniel (June, 1953–
June, 1954), the EDC had been proposed by governments actively
opposed by the Socialists who had, on the other hand, granted their

[40] Jacques Isorni, *J.O., Deb., A.N.* (May 11, 1954), p. 2344. Quoted in
Leites, *Images of Power*, I, 75.
[41] Quoted and commented on in Leites, *On the Game of Politics in
France* (Stanford, California, 1959), pp. 53–54.
[42] Pierre Mendès-France, *J.O., Deb., A.N.* (Dec. 23, 1954), p. 6814.

full backing to Mendès-France. So that, in Nathan Leites' words, "the National Assembly's decision in favor of the country's entering, for an indeterminate period, into the WEU could be presented as a commitment to the Prime Minister of the moment, a commitment that was 'very fragile and precarious' since the man in question was on his way out when the decision was being made." [43] An issue involving a lasting and formal entanglement of France with Europe was therefore decided in terms of the momentary relationship between a given government and the Assembly at a given time.

In other instances, the National Assembly would merely follow its own course and eventually devise a great design in no way related to that of the government. Pierre Mendès-France, an adversary of the Common Market, was prompt to emphasize that "those who are going to vote for the Common Market do not hide—in private conversations, of course—that once we have entered it, our first concern will be to ask the new international organization for an authorization to do all the things the common market forbids its members to do . . . For, while they believe that the treaty, were it to be applied, would be very dangerous, they also foresee . . . that it will not be really applied." [44] The Assembly would thus adopt a given policy merely for the time being (in the most literal sense of that expression). The existing government could not be charged with the responsibility of that policy, since, in all likelihood, it would not live long enough to follow it through. And the succeeding government would not rush its implementation since it did not even initiate it. The EDC, of course, was the best example of such a procedure. Once accepted as a whole, the treaty was ignored by successive governments while it was emptied of its substance through endless additions by the parties of so-called preliminary conditions. Yet, as a vivid symbol of the way the National Assembly defined its role, the EDC was afterward described by a

[43] Leites, *Images of Power*, I, 126.
[44] *L'Express*, July 5, 1957. Quoted in Leites, *On the Game of Politics*, p. 56.

respectable deputy (P. O. Lapie) as "a crisis, the intensity of which . . . did honor to Parliament." [45]

The Assembly did not display any bad faith toward the government, nor did it want to embarrass it *vis-à-vis* the Allies' respective governments. The simple fact was that its interpretations of the policy offered were different from those of the government and the Quai d'Orsay.

Concerning the EDC, for instance, many deputies thought that the treaty had to be ratified in order to provoke Moscow into offering adequate concessions that would assure the success of a hypothetical Four-Power conference. Such a conference would then permit the French Senate (then known as the Council of the Republic) to refuse the ratification of a project which led to the rearmament of Germany. In turn, the Assembly could retract a consent which it had previously granted. The ratification of an agreement was therefore not necessarily conducive to its implementation.

It was obviously difficult for a government in such a position to devise a coherent foreign policy and, whenever devised, to implement it. With every government described as a caretaker government, and every year regarded as a year of transition, the Fourth Republic itself was a Republic of transition, and even the well-known continuity of the heads of personnel at the Quai d'Orsay could not prevent *immobilisme* from eating at the conduct of foreign affairs. During his first try for governmental investiture, Mendès-France had made clear that "France's foreign policy will, in the last analysis, be determined by her internal reorganization." [46] But for such a reorganization to be undertaken, a new Republic was needed.

The Fourth Republic had a history of painful decline which began and ended with a statement of powerlessness. During the years of underground fighting, the French people had suddenly realized "in a flash of lucidity, impartiality, and complete personal detach-

[45] P. O. Lapie, *J.O., Deb., A.N.* (July 11, 1956), p. 3373.
[46] Speech of June 3, 1953, reproduced in *L'Année Politique, 1953*, pp. 490–98.

ment . . . the mistakes [they] had made and the evils [they] had allowed to become deep rooted and chronic." [47] They knew that France had "lost her force and her sway for a long time to come" but were convinced that she was "calmly and surely preparing out of the ruins to relive the course of her entire history and to take her chance in a game where she held no trumps." [48] Yet, the game itself would be played this time "not for power but for justice; not for politics but for ethics; not for the domination of France but for her grandeur." [49]

Instead of the revolution of justice, however, the Fourth Republic brought the restoration of the great division between the powerful and the underprivileged, as prices continued to climb in an endless spiral of inflation, as black markets proliferated, scandals multiplied, and successive governments remained unable to cope with the situation. Instead of the revolution of ethics came the restoration of politics as the Third Republic, in spite of having been rejected at the referendum of October, 1945, by 96.4 per cent of the voters, re-emerged in the Fourth Republic where "the new faces which appear everywhere are eclipsed by the old ones. The troupe is renewed after a long intermission, but the first roles have not changed." [50]

As for the restoration of France's grandeur, career diplomat Alfred Fabre-Luce expressed it best: "Satellites of Washington to avoid being satellites of Moscow, but searching still for a formula for liberation, we dream today of a united Europe, that is to say,

[47] Jules Romains, *A Frenchman Examines His Conscience* (London, 1955), p. 9.

[48] Albert Camus, *Première Lettre à un Ami Allemand* (Paris, 1948), pp. 31–32.

[49] Albert Camus, *Combat* (Aug. 24, 1944), in *Actuelles*, Vol. ii (Paris, 1953), p. 21. "Politics had become a family matter," writes Simone de Beauvoir in her moving account of the "orgy of brotherhood" which she saw in the liberation of Paris. *Force of Circumstance* (New York, 1964), pp. 4ff.

[50] Jacques Fauvet, *La IVème République*, p. 54. By January, 1947, the four national presidencies—of the Republic, the Assembly, the Council of the Republic, and the Council of Ministers—belonged to politicians who had been active under the Third Republic—Vincent Auriol, Edouard Herriot, Auguste Champetier de Ribes, and Paul Ramadier, respectively.

of another foreign influence—a little less foreign." [51] The restoration of France's rank was impossible without a lasting reprieve from party politics which would permit the settlement of the outstanding political, economic, and religious issues, a settlement possibly conducive to a major regrouping of the parties. Once her political system was stabilized, France could move forward in the field of foreign policy and take advantage of some of the major developments recorded between 1945 and 1958—namely the Franco-German *rapprochement* and the foundation of some form of European unity. In other words, the decline of France had to be checked from within, before an ascendant France could be heard in the world without.

[51] "A l'Ombre de la Constitution," *Le Monde*, Nov. 5, 1952. Quoted in Edgar S. Furniss, *Weakness in French Foreign Policy-Making* (Princeton University, Center of International Studies, Memorandum No. 5, February, 1954), p. 49.

PART II

FRANCE ASCENDING

✤

✤ ✤ ✤ ✤

# CHAPTER FIVE

# THE CONDITIONS OF ASCENDANCY

✤ ✤ ✤ ✤ ✤

## I

The coming to power of de Gaulle did not mean a new foreign policy. On the contrary, the Gaullist government repeatedly denied any innovation or desire for it. This attitude, of course, corresponded to a natural inclination to preserve or promote a national consensus, already much affected by the uncertain origins of the new regime, as well as by the persistent Algerian conflict. While preaching major reforms at home, the Fifth Republic emphasized diplomatic continuity. "You have begun, we are merely continuing your work," de Gaulle once told former Foreign Minister Robert Schuman apropos of the Franco-German *rapprochement*.[1] Similarly, the atomic policy of France was linked by the then Premier Michel Debré to all the governments of the Fourth Republic;[2] while the policy of building Europe was, according to Foreign Minister Couve de Murville in 1962, almost ten years old.[3]

In April, 1963, reviewing his high policy, de Gaulle reminded his auditors that it would be impossible "to conduct and lead such an enterprise if we were to spend our time in political divisions

---

[1] André Passeron, *De Gaulle Parle, 1958–1962* (Paris, 1962), p. 433.
[2] *J.O., Deb., A.N.* (Oct. 13, 1960), p. 2512.
[3] French Embassy, *Speeches and Press Conferences*, No. 176 (May 31, 1962).

and social conflicts." [4] To a large extent, political bickering was prevented by national bitterness against former institutions. However divided opinion over events pertaining to May 13, 1958, a consensus had nevertheless emerged against the Fourth Republic, a consensus which, in effect, was in the making in 1946 when the new regime had been approved by only one-third of the electorate, while another third rejected it and the remaining third ignored it. Obviously, it would have been difficult to engage in a dispute over the nature of institutions which were no longer wanted.[5] Furthermore, it was generally agreed that the situation in Algiers created exceptional circumstances which required exceptional measures. In other words, the new regime was provided with a reprieve from partisan politics during which it could undertake salutary adjustments as a prerequisite to the return of domestic stability to which de Gaulle devoted most of the first four years of his stay in power. These, in turn, placed the French government in a position to consider and deal with the problems, not in a slow and changeable way but as a continuous design and a long-range decision.[6]

## II

Soon after the investiture of the Fifth Republic, it was written that "a regime dependent upon one man as much as the Fifth Republic depends upon General de Gaulle is fundamentally in a precarious position." [7] The new regime, it was then argued, would

[4] Address held at Sedan on Apr. 22, 1963. *De Gaulle Parle, 1962–1966*, p. 76.
[5] A poll taken in January, 1958, reported that 52 per cent of the public would have remained indifferent to a military coup, and 44 per cent to a Communist coup. Respectively 4 per cent and 9 per cent of those questioned answered that they would have actively opposed either one of these coups. *Sondages*, 1958, No. 3. Quoted by Pierre Fougeyrollas, *La Conscience Politique dans la France Contemporaine*, p. 158.
[6] Press Conference held on Jan. 14, 1963; *French Embassy, Major Addresses, Statements and Press Conferences of General Charles de Gaulle*, p. 208.
[7] Raymond Aron, *France, Steadfast and Changing*, p. 136.

either evolve into a dictatorship because of the unusual amount of power gathered by its President, or it would create such a vacuum under de Gaulle that only an anarchic situation could succeed him. Still in 1965, Hubert de Beuve-Méry, writing in Le Monde under his usual pen name, Sirius, warned that "any regime abusively personalized, be it the best or the least bad, leads to difficult and sometimes tragic aftermaths, just as much as do those disorderly regimes which it desires to remedy." [8]

"Not a regime, nor even a constitution, but a man" [9]—the Fifth Republic has thus been strongly criticized for the narrow, individual basis on which it seemingly rests. Yet, the problem of personalization of power is peculiar neither to France in general nor to the Fifth Republic in particular. Indeed, in other Western European countries as well as in the United States, democratic regimes have known an acute recrudescence of personalization at a time when the totalitarian regimes of the East display their liberalization by denouncing the principle of a cult of power.[10]

Moreover, the French political consciousness has frequently emerged as a national consensus against parties and institutions. For example, these were judged responsible for "l'anarchie" in 1799, "le désordre" in 1851, "la décadence" in 1940, and "l'immobilisme" in 1954 and 1958. In most cases, this national consensus crystallized in the form of an individual whose role consisted perhaps less in solving the particular problems which contributed to the over-all situation than in restoring France's rank.[11] "Whenever I write de Gaulle's name," noted François Mauriac shortly before

[8] "Simplifications Préélectorales," Le Monde Hebdomadaire, Apr. 29–May 5, 1965.

[9] "L'Avenir de la Cinquième," Le Monde, Jan. 2, 1962.

[10] See Albert Mabileau, "La Personnalisation du Pouvoir dans les Gouvernements Démocratiques," Revue Française de Science Politique, Vol. X, No. 1 (March, 1960), pp. 39–65. Mabileau emphasizes the distinction between personalization and individualization of power: the latter destroys the constitutional framework, whereas the former fits itself within this framework. But the anti-Gaullists argue that de Gaulle ignores the constitutional framework altogether. See also, Léo Hamon and Albert Mabileau (eds.), La Personnalisation du Pouvoir (Paris, 1964).

[11] Pierre Fougeyrollas, La Conscience Politique, pp. 178–89.

the General's return to power, "it is not with the idea that he will save everything . . . But he would give us back honor, and we are dying from a betrayed vocation." [12] What is unique in the Gaullist phenomenon, however, is the nature of the Gaullist consciousness itself, which a French political analyst has aptly described as a partisan anti-partisan consciousness.[13] As an anti-partisan consciousness, the triumph of what is national obviously requires the decline of what is partisan. As such, it confirms de Gaulle's well-known statement according to which "every Frenchman has been, is, or will be a Gaullist." At the same time, the necessity to oppose the parties more effectively makes it indispensable to promote the partisan existence of a political organization. To this extent, then, it is also possible for every Frenchman to have been, to be, or to become an anti-Gaullist.

Furthermore, the Gaullist consciousness distinguishes itself from other such national phenomena by the personality of its leader. Successively, or at times simultaneously, identified with Joan of Arc, Richelieu, Louis XIV, Napoleon I, and Napoleon III, Charles de Gaulle attributes to himself "French . . . legality . . . conferred . . . by the nation." [14] He is accepted—actively or by default—as France, and his interests are thus assimilated to those of France. As Georges Pompidou put it, speaking of the Franco-German Treaty, "Who can believe that this treaty is contrary to the best interests of France when it is signed: de Gaulle?" [15]

On November 4, 1965, when announcing his candidacy for the Presidency, de Gaulle warned the French people that the future of France could be secured only by a frank and massive endorsement of his bid for power. "Otherwise," he went on, "no one could doubt that [the Republic] will crumble at once and that France will have to suffer . . . a confusion of the State still more disastrous than ever before." [16] The paradox of the Gaullists' posi-

[12] *Bloc Notes, 1952–1957*, Feb. 24, 1958, p. 29.
[13] Fougeyrollas, *La Conscience Politique*, p. 139.
[14] *French Embassy, Major Addresses* (Apr. 23, 1961), p. 126.
[15] Georges Pompidou, *J.O., Deb., A.N.* (June 13, 1963), p. 3351.
[16] Address held on Nov. 4, 1965; Passeron, Vol. 2, *De Gaulle Parle*, pp. 122–23.

tion is that they argue for both the perfection of the new institutions and the indispensability of their leader. Here too, this attitude is the outcome of an identification between national and Gaullist consciousness: the former cannot survive the latter which, in turn, is expressed in terms of the former. The political risks inherent in opposing the national aspect of Gaullism makes the opposition reluctant to debate the short-term validity of such identification. What is debated instead are its long-term consequences over the stability of the French political system. "The best proof of the failure of Gaullism," remarked François Mitterand, de Gaulle's chief opponent in the presidential elections of December, 1965, "is the candidature of the General," [17] as he saw in this candidacy the reflection of the vacuum which existed under de Gaulle: "The General has failed to such an extent that nothing will survive his tenure in power. He is running for the presidency because he is the only hope for Gaullism." [18] Yet, de Gaulle is as indispensable to the opposition as he is to the Gaullist party itself. In 1958, the national consensus was built around one man against the prevailing institutions. The same man can now promote a return to partisan consciousness by making the opposition unite against him within the existing political framework. From the viewpoint of the opposition as well as from that of the majority, if de Gaulle did not exist, he would have to be invented.

## III

Obviously, the mirage of political stability, if indeed there is one, cannot depend solely on de Gaulle's personal identification with the present regime. The choice which France faces is neither

[17] *Le Monde*, Oct. 16, 1965.
[18] *Ibid.*, Oct. 26, 1965. Lecanuet also emphasized the same point: "A President of the Republic has no right to say that beyond him the regime ends and France gives up." *Le Monde*, Nov. 6, 1965. And in an editorial of the same day, Sirius pointedly wondered: "What is the meaning of such a reprieve if . . . unavoidable terms condemn us to go to hell?"

between the Fourth and Fifth Republics, as the Gaullists like to put it, nor between the Third and Fourth Republics, as the opposition sometimes replies.[19] The mirage of political stability is bound to depend on the nature of changes introduced by, and associated with, the "Gaullist parenthesis." More explicitly, it rests on the degree to which the residues of France's political life—as they concern isolated issues, the structure of the political parties, and the constitutional question—have faded away or merged into some form of national consensus.

As we have seen, the religious issue, namely the relationship between State and Church in the realm of education, was among the destabilizing problems which the Fifth Republic inherited from the previous regime. Early in 1959, the debate was promptly revived by the Moderates and the MRP who joined forces with the Gaullists to form the same majority which had existed, on this question, in 1951. Yet, at a popular level, the religious debate of 1959 was marked by the moderation of a public undoubtedly concerned with other matters judged more important. At the parliamentary and governmental level, the debate was also characterized by a shared tendency to overlook the ideological nature of the controversy and find a solution which could be accepted by the country at large as satisfactory.[20] Since then, the issue has occasionally been revived by the parties of the left. For example, it was effectively used by Guy Mollet as an obstacle to a formal alliance of the SFIO with the MRP during the politicking that preceded the last presidential elections of December, 1965. Nevertheless, the religious quarrel has now become a side issue which political parties may occasionally use to reopen old wounds, but to which the

[19] The opposition alludes here to the fact that de Gaulle was a Minister during the Third Republic. The exchange was carried one step further during the last legislative elections. Charged by Premier Pompidou with being a man of the Fourth Republic, former Premier Pierre Mendès-France counter-charged Pompidou with being himself a man of the Second Empire. Le Monde, Mar. 1, 1967.

[20] See Aline Coutrot, "La Loi Scolaire de Décembre, 1959," Revue Française de Science Politique, Vol. XIII, No. 2 (June, 1963), p. 364.

public is less and less responsive as the Vatican itself pursues a more and more liberal policy.[21]

From an economic standpoint, the development has been two-fold. General agreement exists on two essential points: first, to combat any further centralization of control and activity in Paris and to bring the centripetal pull of the French capital to an end; second, final adoption of the practice of government planning.[22] This conception of a government armed to act powerfully in the economic domain fits particularly well within the Gaullist framework. The Gaullists find it "incumbent upon the State to create the national power, which henceforth depends on the economy." The latter must therefore be directed, particularly when it is deficient or needs to be renewed, as "it would not be renovated unless the State determines to do so." [23]

Thus, with the exception of the extreme left and a small fraction of the right, an emerging consensus has had to satisfy the requirements of economic modernism. At last, the old debate has lost its formerly rigid and ideological character and has become instead primarily technical. The left has diminished its demands for massive nationalization, collectivism, and state control, while the right has recognized as unavoidable a certain amount of *dirigisme*. Of course, the issue is still occasionally raised. Maurice Duverger, among several others, recently criticized "the policy of . . . de-planning . . . which has deprived the State of many of its means of economic intervention." Yet, he went on to say that "the State

[21] For instance, a recent study prepared by the influential Club Jean Moulin which argued in favor of a regrouping of the forces of the left and center left, asked unequivocally for a definite softening of the Socialist position on the problem of *laïcité*. *Un Parti pour la Gauche* (Paris, 1965).

[22] French planning has been particularly well described by Kindleberger: "French planning is empiricism. The total polity is bent on expansion. This fact is communicated to all corners of the economy, expressed, so far as possible, in terms of numbers . . . Where a sector or industry falls short, one weapon or another may be employed to help." "The Postwar Resurgence of the French Economy," *In Search of France*, p. 155.

[23] De Gaulle, *Mémoires*, III, 116–17.

still has several means of action," reducing the quarrel from one of principle to one of degree.[24]

Early in 1967, labor unrest, followed by a major confrontation between the government and the parties of the left over economic measures, seems to indicate dissatisfaction with the economic policy of the Gaullist government. But the debate centers less on the nature of the economic measures being proposed to the French Assembly than on the political conditions surrounding their adoption. In effect, the economic and social reforms proposed by the government imply a re-endorsement of the goals of the Treaty of Rome—full employment, and modernization or reconversion of industrial sectors or geographical areas threatened by the full implementation of the Common Market (scheduled for July, 1968) or by the consequences of the Kennedy Round.

More controversial, however, are de Gaulle's renewed efforts to promote the association of capital, labor, and technology. In March, 1945, de Gaulle had already offered such a plan: "The workers should be associated with the progress of industries . . . their labors enjoy the same rights as those accorded to capital . . . their remuneration . . . linked, like the revenue of stockholders, to the results of the industry's developments." [25] As in 1945, then, it is likely that the Gaullist program will alienate the left, which might find the measures inadequate, as well as the middle and upper classes, which might find them socialistic.

As to occasional strikes and other periodic expressions of social dissatisfaction they are less a development of great political significance than the spontaneous expression of the French temper. Before January 1956, for instance, France had just experienced three years of a comparable prosperity, characterized by an increase in real wages of 15 to 20 per cent. Yet the elections of that month produced a 40 per cent vote against the system (that is Communist and Poujadist). The fact is that in a period of general prosperity, the average Frenchman remains jealous of his neighbor's well being, so that the least prosperous groups explain their relative failure

[24] *Le Monde,* "L'Etat Désarmé," Feb. 15, 1966.
[25] Quoted in Roy C. Macridis, *De Gaulle, Implacable Ally,* p. 69.

by placing the guilt upon Fate or the State. They then proceed to vote or demonstrate against the regime, even though they might, in any other context, be willing to endorse it.[26]

The Gaullist era has thus witnessed the emergence of a "new sociological France" which is more immune to the ideological quarrels of the past, as a broad accord on a few fundamental options made possible the transcendence of old disputes. Yet, this is obviously not sufficient to transform the mirage of political stability into a reality. Or, in the words of Stanley Hoffmann, "a growing consensus on, or indifference to, the old substantive issues of French politics is not enough to assure political stability." [27] In the last analysis, this stability can only rest on the evolution of parties and institutions.

## IV

Any discussion of the regrouping of political parties in France proceeds from a flagrant paradox, for the Fifth Republic has witnessed an intense multiplication of clubs, associations, committees, etc., amidst a plethora of "fusion, federation, confederation, synthesis, cartel, charter, convention, co-ordination, liaison, co-operation." [28] So, while the government has characterized the *esprit de la Cinquième République* as a constant effort to eliminate at all levels of public life the regime of parties,[29] and the opposition has approvingly spoken of a simplification of political life,[30] which would reflect the wishes of the public for the most part favorable to some role for the parties provided that they regroup,[31] an inventory of political clubs shows that there were forty-five

[26] Raymond Aron, *Steadfast and Changing*, p. 37.

[27] *In Search of France*, p. 99.

[28] Pierre Vianson-Ponte, *Le Monde*, Mar. 3, 1966.

[29] Georges Pompidou, News Conference of Mar. 9, 1965, quoted in *L'Année Politique*, 1965, p. 19.

[30] Guy Mollet. Quoted in *Le Monde*, Sept. 12–13, 1965.

[31] Polls taken in December, 1962. Published in *Revue Française de Science Politique*, Vol. XIII, No. 2 (June, 1963), pp. 430–31.

such organizations by mid-1964.[32] This may have led de Gaulle to reflect: "What is to be feared, in my mind, after the event about which I am speaking [his political disappearance] is not a political void but rather an overflow." [33]

Nevertheless, these clubs indicate hardly any tendency to develop as permanent political forces. Most of them originated after 1958 as a reaction against an assumed depoliticization of French society under the Gaullist regime, and it is probable that their influence, if any, will fade away as signs of a political revitalization become more evident.[34] This seems to be the opinion of as strong a supporter of the concept of political clubs as Charles Hernu: "The day when there is a great movement of enthusiasm, or an exceptional event . . . all these tendencies will regroup in a large political party." [35] Furthermore, lasting or not, these clubs did not prevent real simplification of competing tendencies. In March, 1965, for instance, in the large French towns, there was an average of four electoral lists as compared to seven to ten for the municipal elections of March, 1959.[36] In March, 1967, the parliamentary elections were decided in over 80 per cent of the political districts by a direct contest between a Gaullist and a leftist.

A second preliminary remark should emphasize also that any such regrouping engendered during the Fifth Republic might only be a temporary coalition against one man, rather than a real fusion around a common program. Speaking of a possible "grand alliance" with the Communist party, Guy Mollet recalled that the Socialists were becoming "neither Communist nor reactionary. We do

[32] *Revue Politique et Parlementaire*, No. 747 (August, 1964), pp. 84–92.

[33] Press conference held on May 15, 1962; *French Embassy, Major Addresses*, p. 184.

[34] After the 1965 presidential elections it was suggested that "depoliticization, provided that it ever existed, is now completely over." *L'Année Politique, 1965*, p. 115.

[35] *Revue Parlementaire et Politique*, "Pourquoi des Clubs?" No. 746 (June, 1964), p. 11. Hernu, a fervent *Mendésiste* and actual President of the *Club des Jacobins*, in effect dreams of Gaullism to be succeeded by *Mendésisme*. See also, Club Jean Moulin, *Un Parti pour la Gauche*.

[36] *L'Année Politique, 1965*, p. 18.

not want to please everyone: we just want to defeat the UNR." [37]
These words were confirmed six months later by another Socialist,
Jules Moch: what matters, he said, is "to defeat de Gaulle, far
more than to bring a Socialist to the Presidency." [38] It is for the
same reason, what François Mitterand described as "an incompatibility of character between de Gaulle and democracy," [39] that the
Communist party agreed to endorse a common candidate of the left
on the basis not of a common program but of an acceptable platform.[40] In effect, such tactical coalitions were common during the
Third and Fourth Republics. For example, the 1956 electoral alliance between the Socialists and the Radicals, the *Front Républicain*, largely approved by the voters, soon crumbled in the National Assembly to become a parliamentary alliance of the center
or even of the right. To be lasting, any alliance between political
parties must seek not only a defeat of Gaullism, but also offer an
alternative, while securing definite means to implement that alternative.[41]

A *regroupement* of the parties might take three forms. First of
all, there could be a consolidation and enlargement of the Gaullist
movement. The UNR, to which neither the President of the Republic nor the Prime Minister officially belongs, even though
Georges Pompidou now describes himself as the majority leader,[42]
has repeatedly tried to divorce itself from strict obedience to the
government in order to reflect better the wishes of public opinion.
One of its main leaders, Jean-Jacques Chaban-Delmas, expressed
the consensus of the party when he stated: "The UNR must act
in such a way that its faithfulness does not inhibit its initiative . . .
It must both follow de Gaulle and precede him." [43] In effect, the

[37] *Ibid.*, p. 6.
[38] *Ibid.*, p. 57.
[39] *Le Monde*, Sept. 11, 1965. Actually, the formula was first used by Léon
Blum in 1946. Quoted in Elgey, *La République des Illusions*, p. 63.
[40] *Le Monde*, Sept. 19–20, 1965.
[41] Maurice Duverger, "La Règle du Jeu," *Le Monde*, Sept. 29, 1965.
[42] *Ibid.*, Jan. 15, 1966.
[43] UNR. Congress, November, 1959. Quoted in *Revue Française de
Science Politique*, Vol. XIII, No. 2 (June, 1963), p. 434.

UNR is very hopeful that fear of the Communist party will encourage the parties of the center and the right to join it. This is the Gaullist version of a true center party: "to realize, with our allies of today and with those of tomorrow, a new political formation, larger, wider, and open to all those who believe in a rejuvenated democracy." [44] But the goal of the UNR is frustrated by de Gaulle's diplomatic designs, as it remains difficult to awaken the French people to an imaginary threat of the domestic Communist party while the General praises the Franco-Russian détente.

To a large extent, the UNR suffers the same problem as the MRP faced twenty years ago: being a majority party before being a party at all. To establish its identity, the UNR must maintain a certain distance between itself and de Gaulle, but in order to keep its majority it must tighten the bonds which tie the party to the General. In 1962, the UNR vote represented only 51 per cent of the votes favorable to de Gaulle at the referendum of the previous month.[45] Its goal is obviously to raise this figure, and when seeking alliances to the right and the center right, the UNR responds to its natural vocation and seeks an integration inside the political system, independent of de Gaulle.[46] At any rate, it cer-

[44] Statement made by Roger Frey, then Minister of the Interior, on Feb. 28, 1965. Quoted in *L'Année Politique, 1965*, p. 16. The main problem for Gaullism is less to increase its support from the left than to recover the votes from the center, which abstained in November, 1962, or went to Lecanuet in December, 1965. The identification by the electorate of Gaullism and the center was well shown in the second round of the legislative elections of November, 1962, when the UNR was all the more victorious as its opponent was further away from the center. So, François Goguel has tabulated that out of 87 duels against the Communist party, the UNR won 73 (83.9 per cent). It won 30 out of 57 duels with the SFIO (55 per cent), and only 6 out of 21 with the Radicals (28.5 per cent). *Le Référendum d'Octobre et les Elections de Novembre 1962* (Paris, 1965), *passim*.

[45] François Goguel, "Le Référendum du 28 Octobre et les Elections des 18–25 Novembre 1962," *Revue Française de Science Politique*, Vol. XIII, No. 2 (June, 1963), p. 305.

[46] A recent poll showed that 54 per cent of the electorate regards the UNR as belonging to the political right, and 22 per cent describe it as a party of the center, while only 4 per cent place a leftist label on it, and 19 per cent are uncertain. *Ibid.*, p. 432.

tainly fares better than the former Gaullist party (RPF) which was never either a party or a majority.

The other forms of regrouping relate to various efforts undertaken by opposition parties. These efforts actually are part of an old trend of French politics. Under both the Third and the Fourth Republics, there was a gradual movement of the parties of the left toward the center as the emergence of political organizations on their left wing pushed the Thiers party of the early Third Republic, then the Radicals and the Socialists, toward the center. From this transformation derives the particular nature of French centrism which arises out of the split between the extreme and the moderate factions within the same political wing, thereby leading to an *entente* between the moderates of the left and of the right to obtain a governmental majority, known as a Third Force.[47] This coalition was particularly popular under the Fourth Republic after the failure of Tripartism which included the Communist party in the governmental coalition.

The most dedicated proponent of the constitution of a Third Force is usually the center right party, namely the MRP, all the more so when it faces the phenomenon of national consciousness —in this case Gaullism—be it that of the old RPF or of the present UNR. Unable to face the Gaullist movement endorsed by a major fraction of its usual electoral clientele, the MRP must naturally regard the Gaullist *raz-de-marée* and the rise of the Gaullist party as a temporary phenomenon.[48] It looks for a formula that would enable the party to wait for "the end of an exceptional regime linked to the existence of one man," [49] without, however, complete procrastination. Thus, at home, the MRP is strongly in favor of the creation of a political force which would become the largest

[47] Maurice Duverger, "La Balance ou le Marais?" *Le Monde*, Jan. 7, 1966.
[48] At a poll taken in May, 1964, the MRP sympathizers expressed the following opinions: 58 per cent would vote for de Gaulle; 58 per cent liked his foreign policy; 38 per cent liked his economic policy; 30 per cent liked his social policy. *Revue Française de Science Politique*, Vol. XV, No. 1 (Feb., 1965), p. 68.
[49] Lecanuet, *ibid.*, p. 73.

bloc between the Communist party and the Gaullists. Abroad, it seeks transcendence into a European party. But this constitutes less a regrouping, or a vocation, than an act of self-defense.

During the first half of 1965, efforts were made to realize such a federation under the banner of Gaston Deferre, himself a Socialist.[50] Those efforts failed because the main two members of the projected federation, the MRP and the SFIO, remained divided on three major political issues.[51] First and foremost, the Socialists and the Christian Democrats were unable to agree on the position which the new alliance would adopt *vis-à-vis* the Communist party. The MRP wanted the Communists to remain away from the mainstream of political action, but a majority of the Socialists, led by Guy Mollet in personal opposition to Gaston Deferre, asked for their reintegration into French political life. The second source of opposition concerned the content of the Socialist idea. The MRP wanted to accent the democratic idea that surrounds and determines the Socialist concept and becomes the federative principle of the upcoming federation,[52] thus pushing the Socialists to wonder: "Will this federation be primarily Socialist, in the ideological sense of the term, or will it rest on some form of compromise between Socialist thinking and methods on the one hand, and other forms of action on the other?"[53] Finally, the religious issue was resurrected by the SFIO. While the MRP carefully avoided mentioning it, and despite Deferre's demands that the clerical problem not be presented as a *préalable au regroupement*, Guy Mollet bit-

[50] A good account of Deferre's efforts can be found in William G. Andrews and Stanley Hoffmann, "France: The Search for Presidentialism," *European Politics: The Restless Search*, ed. W. G. Andrews (New York, 1966), pp. 106ff.

[51] See the reports of the national Congress of the MRP (May 27–29, 1965) and of the SFIO (June 3–6, 1965) in the respective issues of *Le Monde*.

[52] *L'Année Politique, 1965*, p. 50.

[53] *Ibid.*, p. 37. In other words (in this case those of Guy Mollet), the SFIO was ready "to melt into a larger ensemble . . . provided that it was a socialist ensemble." *Le Monde*, Apr. 9, 1966.

terly insisted: "*laicité* now appears as a shameful illness of which nothing should be said." [54]

The initiative of Gaston Deferre amounted to the search for a regrouping of the French center. Ultimately, its success depended upon the existence of centripetal forces which would move the moderates of each political wing together by pulling the extremes away. But, on one side, the disappearance of the reactionary right after the elections of November, 1962, has isolated the Gaullist party as the only true force of the right—and Gaullism itself is mainly identified with the center right. And on the other side, the split between the Socialists and the Communists has been considerably narrowed by economic and social transformations, the end of decolonization, the lessening of Cold War tensions, and the toning down of formerly irreconcilable Communist positions toward one-party government, European unity, and the Atlantic Alliance.

Unable to find these centripetal forces within the political spectrum, the center must therefore find them outside of it. Hence the emphasis on the European question, whose possibilities as a cementing factor are obviously dubious. In other words, the development of a center that would preserve its identity from the right supposes first, the disappearance of Gaullism, and second, the reappearance of the antagonism between the Socialists and the Communists. As both prospects look dim, so does the future of a large center *à la Deferre*. The only regrouping of this sort still foreseeable might lead to an enlarged center right party, from Lecanuet to Giscard d'Estaing, present Gaullists included. But it is conditioned on de Gaulle's withdrawal and the solidity of an early agreement on his *dauphin*.

On the left, the regrouping takes the form of a "Fédération de la Gauche Démocratique et Socialiste," broadly described as a "fusion of all the organizations from the democratic left into one single party." [55] The Federation is in effect the outcome of the SFIO's

[54] *L'Année Politique, 1965*, p. 47.
[55] Charter of the Federation, Sept. 15, 1965. Quoted in *L'Année Politique, 1965*, p. 66.

desire to regroup all socialist dissidents, but also of the aversion shown by many Radicals to be enclosed into too unrewarding a dialogue with the MRP and the Independents. There is a common program mostly based upon the seven options and the twenty-eight propositions which François Mitterand presented during the presidential campaign.

Actually, the main problem for the French left is the Communist party. Alone, the Federation cannot obtain a majority, with or without the competition of Gaullism. But a political alliance with the Communists is prevented by a basic inability to define a common program. The SFIO and the rest of the non-Communist left still find unacceptable the Communist platform and the strong dependence of the party upon Moscow. Even the electoral alliance concluded in 1966 was no more than a formalization of past procedures: during the legislative elections of 1962, the SFIO and the Communist party opposed one another in three cases only.[56] However, it would be fallacious to conclude with Jacques Fauvet that the drama of the Federation is that it has no electoral future without the Communist votes, and no governmental future without Lecanuet's votes.[57] Since the Fourth Republic, the extremes of France's political spectrum can be described neither as revolutionary nor as reactionary. The electoral future of the alliance between the Federation and the Communist party was enhanced by de Gaulle's visit to Moscow. The renewal of a Franco-Russian alliance, for example, might later promote the governmental future of the left, the Communist party included.

Even though conventions succeed one another with no apparent concrete result, and despite the presence still of a dozen parties, there is nevertheless little doubt that an evolution toward the creation of large and loose political formations of the American type is now taking place in France. In fact, there are presently no more than four political families remaining: a collectivist left, namely

[56] This was during the second round of the elections. See Jacques Fauvet, "Regroupements et Élections," *Le Monde*, Feb. 8, 1966.
[57] "Le Choix de la Fédération," *Le Monde*, May 10, 1966.

the Communist party, whose reintegration in French political life is closely associated with the thawing of the Cold War; a left of the center, namely the present Federation, still battling the old bureaucracy of the SFIO and advocating economic and social reforms; a right of the center, the Lecanuet faction, broadly liberal and reputedly European; and finally, a right wing, namely the UNR, nationalist and presently authoritarian. Following de Gaulle's departure, these last two families might eventually fuse into a large center party, possibly a majority party, which would leave France with the three political ensembles which Maurice Duverger first anticipated several years ago.[58]

## V

Controversy over political regimes has been a traditional element of France's political life. "In France," writes Jacques Fauvet, "the opposition does not satisfy itself with the criticism . . . of policy, the composition, even the nature of the government. It also . . . proposes to modify the regime . . . May the opposition be from the extreme right or from the extreme left, it is anti-constitutional."[59] Since May, 1958, the real problem of the controversy which has opposed Gaullists and anti-Gaullists has not been to keep the General, or, if at all possible, to chase him away. It has been instead the future of the regime instituted by the Constitution of the Fifth Republic.

At the root of the debate is whether or not the new institutions assure the effectiveness and the continuity of the public powers.[60] While seemingly endowed with the traditional features of parliamentary regimes (responsibility of the government to the parlia-

[58] "Rassemblements et Fantômes," *Le Monde*, May 2, 1963.

[59] *La France Déchirée*, p. 73.

[60] For a text of the constitution of October, 1958, see *Constitutions and Constitutionalism*, ed. William G. Andrews (New York, 1961). The constitution is concisely discussed by Maurice Duverger in "Les Institutions de la Cinquième République," *Revue Française de Science Politique*, Vol. IX, No. 1 (March, 1959), pp. 101–35.

ment), the French Constitution differs from other parliamentary constitutions by its reliance on a double executive, namely the President of the Republic and the President of the Council (or Prime Minister). Such a division responds to one of the main tenets of de Gaulle's political thought. Thus, according to the General, the Constitution must make possible, in time of crisis, the assertion of "a guide . . . in whom the nation could see beyond its own fluctuations, a man in charge of essential matters and the guarantee of its fate." [61] But beyond such circumstances, when the independence and integrity of France are not threatened, de Gaulle accepts the principles of republican parliamentary government where "government and parliament . . . collaborate, the latter controlling the former and authorized to cause its fall." [62]

As embodied in the Constitution of the Fifth Republic, such a political philosophy immediately raises two potential sources of conflict. First, a conflict might arise between the Prime Minister, supported by a parliamentary majority, and the President of the Republic. Chosen by the President, who also names the members of the Cabinet (Article 8) and presides over the Council of Ministers (Article 9), the Prime Minister needs the full confidence of the President if he is to maintain himself in office. At the same time, however, the Prime Minister is responsible to the Parliament, which can force his resignation (Article 50). The position of the Prime Minister would then be clearly untenable in a situation where the President, elected directly by the people on the basis of a given program, would face an Assembly whose majority, also elected directly by the people, would be of a different political complexion. A guarantee of effectiveness and continuity as long as the General, or a man of his stature and popularity, remains in power, the Fifth Republic carries otherwise the seeds of its own structural *immobilisme*.

The second source of conflict concerns the scope of the presidential powers. The President of the Republic, who "inspires, guides and animates national action," holds, as we have seen, much

[61] *Mémoires*, III, 280.
[62] *Ibid.*

power over the Prime Minister and the Cabinet. In effect, it is the President who, on the basis of their reports, takes all the important decisions of the State. He can also determine the fate of the Parliament by dissolving it, or he can even bypass it by engaging a direct monologue of power with the people by way of referendum. Finally, Article 16 invests him, if it should happen that the country and the regime are immediately threatened, with all the duties and all the rights that the public safety involves.[63] Obviously, the powers of the President go far beyond the margins set up in a true presidential regime.

The Gaullists, however, dismiss both problems by denying that they could arise under de Gaulle. Since the General represents the legitimacy of the nation, they argue, there can be no conflict of interest between him and the nation, nor can there be any fear over the limits of his powers. But, as Henry Kissinger puts it, "a structure which can be preserved only if there is a great man in each generation is inherently fragile." [64] Those who defend the regime in the name of its founder are thus precisely those who make unavoidable doubts as to its continuity.

As it now stands, the Constitution of 1958–62 could follow one of three courses. First, it could lead toward a dictatorship, in which case it still leaves the Parliament with too much power. Second, it could lead toward a British type of situation, where a strong government is supported by a clear, well-disciplined majority. But in this case, the powers of the Prime Minister have to be strengthened and the regrouping of parties accelerated. Or third, the Constitution of 1958–62 could lead to a presidential regime, in which case the Prime Minister still holds too much power and the National Assembly not enough. Inherent in these three options is an overall recognition of the need for a strong executive, thus making highly unlikely a return to the practices of the Third and Fourth Republics. This break with past procedures is further promoted

[63] French Embassy, *Major Addresses* (Sept. 20, 1960), p. 191.
[64] U.S., Congress, Senate, Committee on Foreign Relations, *United States Policy toward Europe (and Related Matters)*, Hearings, 80th Cong., 2d sess., 1966, p. 131.

by a broad renewal of the political personnel at the National Assembly. Thus, the 1958 legislative elections witnessed the defeat of 344 incumbent deputies, while sixty-two incumbents did not run again. Before the last legislative elections, out of 465 deputies at the National Assembly, only 148 were there before 1958.[65]

Moreover, the presidential elections of December, 1965, demonstrated a propensity by the survivors of the Fourth Republic to operate realistically within the framework of the new regime and in a way opposed to the tradition of the old one. François Mitterand's early statements according to which the President should not be elected by universal suffrage, at least "as long as there will not have been a regrouping of the political families," [66] or that policies should be made at the National Assembly,[67] were later contradicted by his candidacy and his own program. More recently, the *Centre Démocrate* of Jean Lecanuet reflected this shift toward the endorsement of the present institutions by emphasizing, in its program, that "the institutions of the Fifth Republic are the institutions of France. They belong neither to a man nor to a party." [68]

Nevertheless, the present regime does not solve the problem of effectiveness because it does not solve the problem of the executive (*who* is going to do what?). It does not solve the problem of continuity either because it does not solve the problem of majority (*how* is he going to do what?). Direct election by the people does not create a consensus, it presupposes it. If the electorate must choose between only two men running for the Presidency, a majority—whatever its size—will obviously emerge in favor of one or the other. But that very majority will then disintegrate when it has to choose from among the many parties which might compete at the subsequent legislative elections. A parliamentary majority of coalition, based upon the traditional partisan consciousness of the French electorate, could thus hold different views from those

[65] Pierre Viansson-Ponte, "L'Opposition devant l'Echéance," *Le Monde*, Oct. 21, 1965.
[66] Sept. 21, 1965. Quoted in *L'Année Politique, 1965*, p. 79.
[67] *Ibid.*, p. 80.
[68] *Le Monde*, Feb. 22, 1967.

held by the President, whose majority would be based on the momentary expression of the national consciousness of that same electorate.

Dissolution of the legislature by the President might be the only solution to a conflict of this sort. Some people in France have even suggested that the dismissal of the government by the Assembly be linked with an automatic system of dissolution.[69] But the risks of popular repudiation are obviously great. A ministerial crisis would occur because of a weakening of the presidential majority. To undergo new elections at this time might weaken it still further and place the President in the same position as President MacMahon who, after his ill-timed dissolution of the Assembly in 1873, had to submit to Premier Gambetta's majority or resign from office. A dissolution of the Assembly might also lead to more instability, or what former Premier Michel Debré calls "bad elections," because of the disunity of the opposition.[70] A good case in point was provided during the Fourth Republic by the legislative elections of 1956: called after Edgar Faure had dissolved the Parliament, they gave rise to the impossible "hexagonal Chamber."

On the other hand, the dissolution of the Assembly could be itself accompanied by the automatic resignation of the President. As the threat of new elections would deter the Assembly from sponsoring ministerial crises too frequently, it would also deter the President from too frequent dissolutions. But the electorate might simply decide to re-elect the same majorities, in which case the problem would have been left, at best, unchanged.

It appears that after de Gaulle, the effectiveness and the continuity of the regime will be linked to the emergence of a real constitutional source of decision making. Either the President or the Prime Minister must become the main source of executive power through the transformation of the present system into either a true presi-

[69] See Jean-Luc Parodi, "Quatre Années de Controverse Constitutionelle," *Revue Française de Science Politique*, Vol. XII, No. 4 (Dec., 1962), pp. 845–76.

[70] See Michel Debré's answer to Paul Reynaud's letter on the question. *Le Monde*, Jan. 20, 1961.

dential government on the American model (with whatever accommodations that must be made to France's political originality), or a multiparty parliamentary government similar to that existing in some Western European countries. But a debate of this type, supposing that it is not solved in the near future by de Gaulle himself, does not need to imply a return to past instability.

In its initial, national phase, Gaullism helped smooth many of the perennial socio-economic quarrels of the past Republics. Parallel to this development, the French people acquired some of the political maturity commonly associated with the shift from a largely agrarian society to a techno-industrial society. This, in turn, led to the early staging of a polarization of political parties, all of which lean toward the moderate center rather than toward either extreme, right or left. It is once the major problems are solved that the national leadership must become partisan again, at which point it requires a renewed public support to resume, eventually, its national character. The survival of Gaullism depends precisely on its ability to realize these successive transformations. Should it fail to do so, it will be up to the present opposition itself, once back in power, to safeguard the domestic inheritance of the Fifth Republic.

CHAPTER SIX

✠ ✠ ✠ ✠

## THE EFFECTS OF ASCENDANCY

✠ ✠ ✠ ✠ ✠

I

In 1945, when the National Assembly, after having elected a President of the Assembly in the person of Félix Gouin, had to select a Prime Minister, de Gaulle did not deem it necessary to offer his candidature or say anything about his eventual platform. "I would be taken as I was," he later commented, "or I would not be taken at all." [1] In 1958, when the National Assembly was being threatened by a military coup which had originated in Algiers, the content of de Gaulle's platform was not a matter of prolonged debate either. Yet, in the Fifth Republic, when there can be no doubt as to who makes major decisions—and more particularly, decisions regarding matters of foreign policy[2]—the question of de Gaulle's program becomes essential. One of the foremost and most faithful Gaullists, François Mauriac, has written in his biography of de Gaulle: "It is what he already sees that enables de Gaulle to fore-

---

[1] Quoted by Georgette Elgey, *La République des Illusions,* p. 63.

[2] See his press conference of Sept. 9, 1965. Also, W. W. Kulski, *De Gaulle and the World* (Syracuse, New York, 1966), p. 1, and Alfred Grosser, *La Politique Extérieure de la Vème République* (Paris, 1965), p. 25. Yet, de Gaulle's decisions are not taken in a vacuum, as we have been arguing that he did not—indeed could not—inaugurate a foreign policy; a new style, a new impulsion, or a better handling of the problems as they arise—in other words, a renewal as to the means—but certainly not a reappraisal as to the ends.

see." [3] But in determining how de Gaulle views the present and envisions the future, we face the mystique of his complex personality. In a recent book, W. W. Kulski analyzed him as a charismatic leader, i.e., "a man who, together with his followers, believes that he has been called upon by God or by history or by destiny . . . to carry out great feats for the benefit of his nation." [4] Indeed, there is something mythical in de Gaulle, who is closer to a fictitious character than an earthly chief of state. François Mauriac makes the point when he describes his feelings during his first meeting with the General: "I was not sorry, that day, to feel somewhat remote from this strange figure . . . I had invented many characters, but . . . I had never seen one, really seen one with my own eyes." [5]

In many ways, de Gaulle's identification with the extraordinary men of French literature is staggering. For example, the General perfectly embodies features common to the various heroes of some of France's foremost writers, most notable among them André Malraux. Manuel, Kyo, Ferral and Gisors, Garine, Perkins—respectively the main figures in *Man's Hope*, *Man's Faith*, *The Conquerors*, and *The Royal Way*—all are characterized by a need for grandeur, a feeling of tragic loneliness, a constant power of will and disdain. [6] Manuel, for instance, while transforming himself into a chief, becomes "sadder and sadder, tougher and tougher" but at the same time more and more lonely. [7] He consoles himself by reasoning that "to be liked without pleasing is one of the most desirable fates of Man." [8] There is also Ferral who, full of disdain, con-

[3] *De Gaulle* (New York, 1966), p. 99.

[4] *De Gaulle and the World*, pp. 1–2.

[5] *De Gaulle*, p. 7. Actually, this is not the first time that Mauriac mixes fiction and politics. Back in the early fifties, he wrote of François Mitterand: "He is a *garçon romanesque:* I mean to say, a character of a novel." Quoted in *Le Monde* (from Bloc Notes written for *L'Express* in 1954), Sept. 11, 1965.

[6] Simon Serfaty, "Gaullist Myth and French Reality," *SAIS Review*, Vol. VIII, No. 3 (Spring, 1964), pp. 15–21.

[7] *L'Espoir* (Collection Livre de Poche; Paris, 1947), p. 400.

[8] *Ibid.*, p. 173.

cludes, "a minority still consists of a majority of idiots." [9] Gisors' description of Man is quite similar to that of a modern commentator's analysis of the General. "He does not want to govern, he wants to constrain . . . to be more than a man in a world of men . . . not powerful but omnipotent . . . each man dreams of being God." [10]

This striking similarity between de Gaulle and Malraux's heroes is accentuated by the similarity to the setting within which they must act. What is debated in Malraux's novels is the conflict of man and the system—conflict of the peasants with the established regime in *Man's Hope*, or of Kyo and Marxism in *Man's Faith*. Similarly, the endless struggle faced by de Gaulle is with the system, that of the parties or that of Yalta, in the face of which he must preserve his moral integrity.

There are three main themes, or realities, in de Gaulle's vision. First, human affairs are seen as leading inevitably toward struggle and conflict. Nations constantly contest for hegemony to which they aspire, whatever their avowed ideology, nature, and propaganda.[11] Facing such a belligerent world, nations need power, not only to flourish, if they can, but also to survive, which they must. According to de Gaulle, life cannot be conceived without force, in the absence of which "thought would have no driving power, action no strength." [12] Yet, ultimately—the rule of all rules is for the nation to survive. To ensure its survival "in a world always full of dangers," elementary guarantees come from within: "a solid State, a modern defense and a united nation." [13] When such guarantees are not sufficient, supplementary guarantees can be found in alliances, but if no guarantee is available at all, a reappraisal of the interests of the nation may then be undertaken, if only for the

[9] *La Condition Humaine* (Collection Livre de Poche; Paris, 1946), p. 69.
[10] *Ibid.*, p. 192.
[11] Press Conference of July 23, 1964, Passeron, *De Gaulle Parle*, Vol. 2, p. 225.
[12] *The Edge of the Sword* (New York, 1940), p. 9.
[13] Address of Aug. 20, 1964. Passeron, *De Gaulle Parle*, Vol. 2, p. 235.

time being, since, whatever the drama, there will be in the future new conjunctures and new opportunities.[14]

Obviously, de Gaulle's view of international relations as a struggle for power and survival is centered on a forceful concept of the nation-state as the only recipient of human endeavor. From Maurras, de Gaulle has borrowed the distinction between the *pays réel*, that of the people, and the *pays légal*, that of institutions.[15] The *pays légal*, the state, is worthy of the *pays réel*, the nation, when it can arise above *parti pris* and party politics and embody the continuity of the national interest. But the originality of Gaullist nationalism is that, unlike Maurras, de Gaulle does not want to be a nationalist against the nation, that is against the most widespread attitude in the nation. Thus, the General's Golden Rule is never to go against a national consensus, real or virtual. In this respect, de Gaulle, called upon by the *pays réel* to personify the *pays légal*, truly wants to represent the legitimacy of the nation.[16] He stands "for the country and with the country." [17]

The nation-state is then the supreme unit of the international system. "Only the states . . . are valid, legitimate and capable of achievement." [18] The fact is that they alone have the right to order and the authority to act in the name of the nation.[19] Any and all other entities may have some technical value, but without the authority to act, none can have any political effectiveness. In this context, ideologies are of little importance, if any. They come and go, as do the ambitions which they help cover under their banners.[20] This is in fact all the more valid in the atomic age, when the threat of ultimate destruction seemingly prevents any formal dogmatism: "many people do not see any reason to trust in ideologies since, in one second, the whole world could be totally annihilated and since,

[14] Address of June 12, 1964, Passeron, *De Gaulle Parle,* Vol. 2, p. 224.
[15] Norman Beloff, *The General Says No* (London, 1963), p. 21.
[16] French Embassy, *Major Addresses* (Apr. 23, 1961), p. 128.
[17] Address of June 12, 1964, Passeron, *De Gaulle Parle,* Vol. 2, p. 96.
[18] Press conference of May 15, 1962, French Embassy, *Major Addresses,* p. 176.
[19] Press conference of Sept. 5, 1960, *ibid.,* p. 93.
[20] Press conference of July 29, 1963, *ibid.,* p. 237.

in these circumstances, great world problems cannot be resolved in a deliberate manner." [21] In the last analysis, it is implicit here that within the international system ideologies play the same negative role as political parties do within the domestic system.

Status within the international community is measured in terms of power. Even though "the past never resumes as it was," [22] it "remains true that in the life of a people each action of the past enters into consideration for the future. There is only one history of France." [23] That history is proof, in de Gaulle's view, that, as a nation, France preserved the talent and habit of grandeur[24] because, "for fourteen centuries, military power [remained her] second nature . . . That our army should outstrip every other army in the world, our fleet be one of the best, our air force of the first order, our generals the most able—that, for us, was only natural." [25] The possession of force is indeed an indispensable prerequisite to all national accomplishments. Force alone has "watched over civilizations in the cradle; . . . ruled empires and dug the grave of decadence; force gives laws to the peoples and controls their destinies." [26] In foreign affairs more particularly, "logic and sentiment do not weigh heavily in comparison with the realities of power." [27] The failure of the Fourth Republic stemmed precisely from its inability to gather enough power to try to impose its policy abroad as well as at home.[28]

Thus, the primary goal of the State is to enhance its power. Eventually, the State and its representatives will be judged according to their contribution to the glory of national defense.[29] For

[21] Press conference of May 15, 1962, *ibid.*, p. 172.

[22] Address of August 20. 1964, Passeron, *De Gaulle Parle*, Vol. 2, p. 235.

[23] Address of September 6, 1964, *ibid.*, p. 239.

[24] French Embassy, *Major Addresses* (May 31, 1960), p. 78.

[25] *War Memoirs*, II (New York, 1959), 276-77. Macridis (ed.), *De Gaulle, Implacable Ally*, p. 130.

[26] *The Edge of the Sword*, p. 10.

[27] *War Memoirs*, Vol. 2, quoted in David Calleo, *Europe's Future* (New York, 1965), p. 114.

[28] Press conference of March 15, 1959, French Embassy, *Major Addresses*, p. 42.

[29] Address of November 3, 1959, in Macridis, *De Gaulle, Implacable Ally*, p. 136.

power is indispensable, not only to maintain one's rank but also to survive in the international community. "International life," says de Gaulle, "like life in general, is a struggle"—a struggle for power, that is,[30] with defense being the ultimate *raison d'être* of the state. "Of all the things which a nation is . . . there is nothing which is more essential than its defense." [31] It follows that "the defense of France must be French . . . It is indispensable that France defend herself by herself, for herself, and in her own way. If it should be otherwise . . . it would not be possible for us to maintain a state," all the more so in France where the "necessities of defense were always at the origin of the State and of the regimes that came into being." [32]

The concept of national survival takes, in de Gaulle's thought, a very ambiguous meaning. One of the General's central themes— "France must be France"—implies a French nation with a personality and a soul as much as an action and a policy.[33] As such, the survival of France goes beyond the physical. Rather than a narrowly conceived territory, it is an idea, a view of France which is to be preserved: "All my life I have had a view of France." [34] To alter this view—a view which in de Gaulle is based on domestic unity and international rank—"would amount to France's giving up, in an attempt to keep her life, her reasons for living." [35] Yet, at times, de Gaulle has displayed a narrower view of France's security: "The national interest is before anything else that of France in France." [36] In this case, the idea of survival becomes obviously entirely physical. And it seemingly is, then, the essential concern of the State.

However preferable, the national nature of defense is not exclusive. If France alone cannot ensure her security, or that of Europe,

[30] French Embassy, *Major Addresses* (May 31, 1960), p. 78.
[31] Address of November 3, 1959, in Macridis, *De Gaulle, Implacable Ally*, p. 135.
[32] *Ibid.*, p. 133.
[33] Address of May 20, 1962, Passeron, *De Gaulle Parle*, Vol. 2, p. 198.
[34] *Mémoires*, I, 1.
[35] Press conference of March 25, 1959, French Embassy, *Major Addresses*, p. 42.
[36] Quoted in Passeron, *De Gaulle Parle*, Vol. 1, p. 410.

then her resources may be combined with those of others. But these alliances, which are the key to de Gaulle's search for a new order, a different equilibrium,[37] need not be integrative. "The alliance will be all the more vital and strong as the Great Powers unite on the basis of a co-operation in which each carries its own load, rather than on the basis of an integration in which peoples and governments find themselves deprived of their roles and responsibilities in the domain of their own defense."[38]

Alliances lead to equilibrium and "it is only in equilibrium that the world will find peace."[39] The *système de Yalta* is destabilizing, as it was imposed upon defeated and weakened powers by the two hegemonies of the time. The equilibrium itself endangers world peace, because it is not based on the realities of power but instead on the fallacies of ideologies.[40] The indispensable condition to the creation of a new balance is then the development of a strong "European Europe," institutionalized along the lines of organized co-operation between States.[41] Close unity on both sides of the Rhine, of the Alps, and perhaps of the Channel will eventually lead to the erection of "the most powerful, prosperous, and influential political, cultural, and economic complex in the world."[42] Such a united bloc, "with sufficient strength, sufficient means, and sufficient cohesion to exist by itself"[43] will make possible, in the shadow of the equilibrium of the two Super Powers, the development of "the understanding, then the co-operation and, finally . . . the osmosis of all the European peoples."[44] It will then be up to Europe to recreate the equilibrium of the world,[45] as the day

[37] Statement of Apr. 29, 1965, *Le Monde Hebdomadaire*, Apr. 29–May 5, 1965.
[38] Address of Nov. 3, 1959, in Macridis, *De Gaulle, Implacable Ally*, p. 134.
[39] French Embassy, *Major Addresses* (May 31, 1960), p. 78.
[40] Statement of Apr. 6, 1965, quoted in Passeron, *De Gaulle Parle*, Vol. 2, p. 107.
[41] French Embassy, *Major Addresses* (May 31, 1960), p. 78.
[42] *Ibid.*, address of Feb. 5, 1962, p. 159.
[43] Press conference of May 15, 1962, *ibid.*, p. 173.
[44] Press conference of Sept. 5, 1961, *ibid.*, p. 142.
[45] Speech of Feb. 11, 1950, quoted in *Le Monde*, Nov. 28–29, 1965.

will have finally come when Europe could play again a determining role as the arbiter of world peace.[46]

"The foreign policy of de Gaulle," wrote Paul Reynaud in a little pamphlet attacking the General, "represents the will of one man." [47] There is no need to deny this. But Paul Reynaud broadly assumes that de Gaulle's will has nothing to do with the will and the desires of the French people. In effect, the belief that de Gaulle's departure—whenever it occurs—will promote a drastic change in the foreign policy of France has been the essential expectation of many of France's frustrated Allies. All things considered, it is difficult to find a sound basis for such expectation. In its essence—not only the attainment of rank but also its exploitation to further security—the Gaullist foreign policy represents a return to a tradition which post-war international conditions, together with the dismemberment of the domestic centers of political power, made unattainable during the Fourth Republic. In its broad lines, the Gaullist foreign policy is widely accepted by a public all in all flattered by the consideration granted to them through the person of their President. This popular consensus in matters of foreign policy is not unnoticed by the political leaders whose substantial criticism is rather scarce. "The broad outline of Mr. Deferre's platform is astonishingly like General de Gaulle's own policy," wrote the *Manchester Guardian* in unseemly stupor at the time of Deferre's presidential candidature.[48] Nevertheless, François Mitterand has contested that de Gaulle's foreign policy will retain any permanent significance,[49] and Lecanuet's conviction is that "when de Gaulle retires, his policy will not be maintained." [50] Yet, their opposition, just as that of the political parties or alliances which they represent, refers to the style rather than to the content of the policy: undoubtedly, de Gaulle expresses much of what is in French minds—past and present—and his policies, which largely continue

[46] Address of May 19, 1962, quoted in *Le Monde*, May 21, 1962.
[47] *The Foreign Policy of Charles de Gaulle*, p. 1.
[48] Issue of Mar. 26, 1964.
[49] *Le Monde*, Oct. 12, 1965.
[50] *Ibid.*, Mar. 24, 1966.

or resume policies adopted before him, will not disappear after him.[51]

Actually, the parties hold the same attitudes as they did during the Fourth Republic. The Socialists and their allies of the left fear the repercussions which French nationalism might have upon Germany's own brand of nationalism. For the most part, they share the Gaullist position toward the Atlantic Alliance and NATO, even though such a position is not judged proper in its form.[52] What is criticized, however, is the absence of a policy of *rechange*. "It is dangerous," they claim, "to disengage ourselves without an engagement somewhere else." [53] Obviously, the alternative policy is that of European unity, particularly as the arrival of Wilson to power meant the revival of old Socialist hopes to have Great Britain enlarge the "small, dark box."

The MRP is all in favor of co-operation with Germany, even though it is fearful of the repercussions which a Paris–Bonn dialogue might have on the cohesion of the European community. Like the Socialists, they want the inclusion of Great Britain and the enlargement of the "little Europe" as a prerequisite to an equilibrium between Europe and the United States. As we move toward the right, however, such pro-British feelings confront a latent approval of de Gaulle's handsome handling of Great Britain: "In no way do we criticize the government for its firmness," noted René Pleven during the debates at the Assembly which followed de Gaulle's news conference of January 14, 1963.[54]

Finally, while the left is staunchly against the force de frappe, judged "inefficient, ruinous, and dangerous," [55] it remains nonetheless true that the French atomic forces originated during leftist

[51] The same conclusion is reached by Kulski, *De Gaulle and the World*, p. 76.

[52] According to Mitterand, "de Gaulle is right in asking for a study and reappraisal [of NATO] but he is wrong to do so in the terms he has chosen and in the tone which is his, notably vis-à-vis the U.S." *Le Monde*, Sept. 23, 1965.

[53] François Mitterand, quoted in *ibid.*, Apr. 16, 1966.

[54] *J.O., Deb., A.N.* (Jan. 25, 1963), pp. 1655–56.

[55] Mitterand, quoted in *Le Monde*, Sept. 23, 1965.

governments. On the right and center right little is said of the issue except that, in Pleven's words, the United States "committed a grave mistake in . . . not helping us to create national forces." [56] But in the words of an opponent of France's nuclear ambitions, the French force de frappe has now become "a political fact, . . . a national and international reality which it is impossible to overlook and which will have . . . to be integrated in post-Gaullist diplomacy." [57]

The opposition seeks the substitution of a wider, European nationalism for the narrow, French nationalism.[58] A political Europe is described by the left as a good way of opposing the strength which the United States derives from European weakness. It is also seen as the only vehicle for an overture to the East.[59] Here too, the Gaullist viewpoint is not fundamentally altered. "As far as nationalism goes," emphasized Foreign Minister Couve de Murville, "I would be quite satisfied to rally myself to European nationalism." [60] In sum, in its broad lines and apart from consideration of methods and style, the post-Gaullist period should be, in the realm of diplomacy, Gaullism without de Gaulle. But to say this would too easily solve a difficulty of manners which is perhaps the most frustrating element of Gaullist diplomacy.

## II

There is a certain dose of Americanophobia in the foreign policy of the Fifth Republic.[61] Even though often denied, de Gaulle's dis-

[56] *Ibid.*, Apr. 16, 1966.

[57] Maurice Faure, "Le Choix de la France," *Le Monde Hebdomadaire*, Feb. 13–19, 1964.

[58] See, for example, André Fontaine, "Une Candidature Européenne," *Le Monde*, Aug. 4, 1965.

[59] François Mitterand, quoted in *ibid.*, Sept. 30, 1965.

[60] *J.O., Deb., A.N.* (Jan. 25, 1963), p. 1663.

[61] The roots of de Gaulle's hostility are particularly well related by Milton Viorst in *Hostile Allies: FDR and Charles de Gaulle* (New York, 1965).

trust of the United States, his forceful repugnance toward any organization where the Anglo-Saxons could have the dominant
voice, is well established.[62] It is never without apparent nostalgia
that the General reminisces, for example, on those heroic times
when, in an open confrontation with the United States, he occupied the islands of Saint-Pierre and Miquelon, formed the liberation
government in North Africa, disapproved of Yalta, and declined
to go to Algiers for a meeting with Franklin D. Roosevelt, who
was then returning from that "deplorable experience." [63] Through
the years, the confrontation never ceased and in the sixties, it can
be recognized in Southeast Asia, the Middle East, and Canada.

Yet, anti-Americanism, as it is found in France, goes far beyond
de Gaulle himself. It was born in the early days of the Fourth Republic as a resentment of dependence—an outlet to a battle against
humiliation then thought to be lost. By bringing into focus the
image of an ascendant France, the Fifth Republic diminished such
feeling as it transformed, in the words of Alfred Grosser, a "nationalism of humiliation" into a "nationalism of prestige and will
power." [64] In the meanwhile, however, anti-Americanism had been
aggravated by the increasingly liberal policy followed by the
United States on colonial matters. Between 1955–56 and 1963,
successive French governments expected—to use Alastair Bu-
chan's phrase—to be treated consistently "rather than to be hailed
as blood-brothers one moment and rabid imperialists the next." [65]
The war in Algeria was widely displayed by France as a struggle
deserving American support, as had Indochina before, since "the
combat is the same and comparable things must be compared." [66]
At any rate, the French government agreed with Michel Debré,
then its prime minister, that "France's policy in Algeria must not

[62] "I am not anti-American," pleaded de Gaulle in December, 1965. Quoted
in Passeron, *De Gaulle Parle*, Vol. 2, p. 249.

[63] Press conference of July 29, 1963, French Embassy, *Major Addresses*,
p. 232.

[64] "Commodités de l'Anti-Américanisme," *Le Monde*, Nov. 25, 1965.

[65] "The Campaign Seen from Europe," *The Reporter*, Vol. 23, No. 7
(Oct. 27, 1960).

[66] Michel Debré, *J.O., Deb., A.N.* (Oct. 13, 1960), p. 2516.

be contradicted by anybody who wishes our alliance." [67] Finally, in its intellectual expression, anti-Americanism has remained based on a fundamental skepticism with regard to the possibilities offered by American civilization. "We must say it, we must write it," reflected Maurice Duverger a few years ago, "there is only one intimate threat for Europe, and that is American civilization." [68]

The label anti-American actually implies too simply that the policy of France must be judged in terms of an American criterion. It is thus as easy for the French to retort that their policy can only be judged in terms of the interest of France, first and foremost, and that, in the words of Couve de Murville, "systematic conformity is not a policy." [69] On the other hand, the French government finds it possible to follow a policy of general co-operation in theory, while denying the possibility of a co-operation with the General in practice. In theory, then, American leadership is accepted, however reluctantly, as "there can be no question that political and military capabilities [of the U.S.] confer upon it certain rights." [70] But the limits of those rights, the limits to inequality, are then described in terms of the balance existing between the American material effort and the European physical risk.[71] Such an argument, somewhat acceptable under the Fourth Republic when the hypothesis of a Soviet attack was still valid, is incompatible with a Gaullist outlook which takes security for granted.

In theory, the Fifth Republic, as the Fourth Republic before it, mildly hails the Atlantic Alliance as the best of the worst systems. According to de Gaulle, there could be no question for France and her Allies of separating from each other as the Alliance remains "indispensable so long as the ambitions and the threats of the Soviets are raised." [72] But in practice, within the Alliance, the

---

[67] Quoted in *Survey of International Affairs, 1959–1960* (Aug. 23, 1959), p. 82.

[68] Quoted in Grosser, *La Vème République*, p. 168.

[69] French Embassy, French Affairs, No. 163, p. 6.

[70] Debré, *J.O., Deb., A.N.* (Oct. 13, 1960), p. 2512.

[71] Press conference of May 15, 1962, French Embassy, *Major Addresses*, p. 178.

[72] Press conference of Jan. 31, 1964, French Embassy, *Major Addresses*, p. 255.

Gaullist government sees a certain military organization which is the real object of its dissatisfaction since it did not evolve according to the circumstances.[73]

The Alliance itself, then, deters a theoretical aggression against the European status quo as it symbolizes the guarantee of an American nuclear retaliation to any such aggression. NATO, the physical embodiment of the alliance, is merely the military organization that takes over once deterrence has failed. It is thus possible to make simultaneously a profession of faith toward the alliance and demands for national defense. The French force de frappe increases the risks of the aggressor by doubling the United States possibility with a French certitude of retaliation. As such, a national defense strengthens the deterrent function of the Alliance.

Where the contradiction lies, however, is in the French insistence upon the uncertain nature of American involvement: should the Soviet Union be convinced by the Gaullist argument, then the credibility of deterrence itself would be unfavorably affected. In April, 1963, for instance, de Gaulle described the United States as "resolved . . . to fight . . . in order to prevent Europe from falling, dead or alive, into the other camp." [74] But in July of the same year, he qualified the U.S. commitment as being naturally based in its timing, amplitude, and modality on one main objective, namely the survival of the United States.[75] Less than a year later, the former "good ally" had become a "foreign protector wholly uncertain." [76] The Gaullist policy then cannot loosen the bonds of NATO without at the same time lessening the effectiveness of the Alliance. Herein lies its first contradiction.

Actually, within the Atlantic Alliance the position of France has always been in doubt. As we have seen, a declining France joined the Western bandwagon as all the other alternatives were

[73] Statement of Dec. 31, 1964. Passeron, *De Gaulle Parle*, Vol. 2, p. 244. See also press conference of May 15, 1962, French Embassy, *Major Addresses*, p. 180.

[74] Press conference of Apr. 19, 1963, *ibid.*, p. 225.

[75] Press conference of July 29, 1963, *ibid.*, p. 235.

[76] Address of April 16, 1964, Passeron, *De Gaulle Parle*, Vol. 2, p. 223.

closed one by one. "To govern," answered de Gaulle to a formula made famous by Pierre Mendès-France, "is to choose between unpleasant alternatives." Obviously, then, the General assumes that the conditions which prevailed in 1949, when he strongly advocated the extension of the Marshall Plan to defense matters, have now been radically changed.[77] "At that time," theorizes de Gaulle, "the burning question . . . was merely the security of Europe. So we made an alliance limited to Europe . . . Furthermore, at that same time, it appeared that the United States alone had the means for defense and that the states of Western Europe . . . found themselves in a political, economic, and social position, of which the best that can be said is that it was uncertain." [78] Yet, since then, "the reasons which, for Europe, made this alliance a form of subordination are fading away day by day." [79] First of all, the French government sees a political transformation in the nature of the East-West conflict as it has evolved from a physical confrontation in Europe into a global, world-wide confrontation. Second, the emergence of polycentric forces is seen as eroding the former cohesion of both blocs. In the East, "the monolithic nature of the totalitarian world is in the process of dislocation." [80] In the West, "the countries of continental Europe, France in particular . . . have regained their balance." [81] Finally, the nature of the military confrontation has been altered: first, when the development of Soviet atomic forces rendered the United States vulnerable to the enemy's reprisals, thereby changing the very meaning of the alliance;[82] second, when France began to build an independent atomic arsenal of her own.[83]

While none of these changes can affect the principle of the alli-

[77] Quoted in Barsalou, *La Mal-Aimée*, p. 97.

[78] Press conference of Sept. 5, 1960, French Embassy, *Major Addresses*, p. 95.

[79] Press conference of July 23, 1964, French Embassy, *Speeches and Press Conferences*, No. 208, p. 5.

[80] Press conference of July 23, 1964, *ibid.*, p. 4.

[81] Press conference of Sept. 5, 1960, French Embassy, *Major Addresses*, p. 96.

[82] Press conference of May 15, 1962, *ibid.*, p. 180.

[83] Press conference of Sept. 5, 1960, *ibid.*, p. 96.

ance itself, they do affect its scope, function, and organization. More specifically, then, the French government requested, shortly after de Gaulle's return to power, the formulation of a global strategy that would be applied to an enlarged NATO area, a redefinition of the notion of automaticity, and a higher degree of co-operation and consultation.[84] These were to be satisfied through the creation of a triumvirate composed of the only three world powers of the Alliance, which would meet regularly to reassess and define global policies. Finally, as these world powers were equal, the French government expected to be treated by the United States in the same way as Great Britain, particularly over the question of ownership and control of nuclear weapons.

The point is often made, however, that the Gaullist reasoning and demands merely aimed at masking a fundamental determination to take France out of the Atlantic Alliance. According to Arthur Schlesinger, for example, very little could have been done by France's allies to divert de Gaulle "from what has plainly been the cherished objective of his life." [85] At a first glance, this assumption—an oversimplified one, as it disregards the fact that most of de Gaulle's demands paralleled the reservations expressed by the National Assembly during the debates of July, 1949, over the adoption of the North Atlantic Treaty—is confirmed by the rejection of the two offers which were made by the Kennedy administration and which would have provided de Gaulle with an opportunity to see his requests at least partly accepted. A first, informal offer was made during Kennedy's visit to Paris in the spring of 1961, when the American President proposed the consideration of a mechanism of consultation, both political and military, among France, Great Britain, and the United States.[86] De Gaulle rejected such a suggestion until the completion of the then forthcoming

[84] Most of these demands were included in the Memorandum of Sept. 24, 1958. For its analysis, see André Fontaine, *L'Alliance Atlantique à l'Heure du Dégel* (Paris, 1959). According to Kulski (*De Gaulle and the World*, p. 166), the memorandum was resubmitted to President Kennedy in a personal letter dated January, 1962.

[85] Arthur Schlesinger, *A Thousand Days* (New York, 1966), p. 867.

[86] *Ibid.*, p. 357.

German elections, and the offer remained a dead letter. "We tried to get down to the brass tacks of discussion," commented Mc-George Bundy later on, "but there was no real willingness in France to discuss the ways and means of such three-power consultation." [87] Yet, Kennedy's offer represented a departure from the basic position of the previous administration: "There have been occasional meetings on a tripartite basis," said Christian Herter (then Secretary of State), but "it has never been institutionalized and we do not expect that it will be." [88]

A second opportunity for an accommodation of differences arose after the Nassau meeting between Kennedy and Macmillan. The offer was then made to de Gaulle, "as an entirely genuine proposal, though made publicly, formally, and without the ceremony the General might have expected" [89] of Polaris submarines on the same terms as to Great Britain—i.e., assignment to NATO but with an escape clause in case of undefined supreme national interests. Furthermore, there was the added possibility of a British offer of Polaris warheads to Paris in exchange for France's nuclear cooperation.

This offer also implied a departure from previously stated policies. In November, 1961, for example, President Kennedy had emphasized that a basic principle of United States policy was "not to give nuclear weapons to any other country." [90] The Nassau plan was thus essentially a success for Gaullist diplomacy, as the equality among the three powers was implicitly recognized, and the triumvirate was established *de principio* if not *de facto*.

But by then, the problems encountered by Great Britain in the development of her own independent nuclear force after the failure of the *Skybolt* project together with the prospect of her entry into the Common Market had led the French government to ex-

[87] McGeorge Bundy, *Hearings*, p. 28.
[88] News conference of Sept. 15, 1960. Quoted in *Survey of International Affairs, 1959–1960*, p. 85.
[89] Schlesinger, *A Thousand Days*, p. 865. Schlesinger's account is fairly well confirmed by André Fontaine, "Histoire de la Force Multilatérale," *Le Monde Hebdomadaire*, Nov. 12–18, 19–25, and Nov. 26–Dec. 2, 1964.
[90] *New York Times*, Nov. 26, 1961.

pect true nuclear co-operation between both countries, a co-operation that would be conducted independently from Washington. As such, then, the Nassau offers were far less than expected. "Mr. Macmillan," de Gaulle said later, alluding to the conversations he had held with the British Premier prior to the Nassau meeting, "has come to tell me that we were right to build our force de frappe. We also have ours, he said, and we ought to be able to unite the two within a context that would be independent from the United States." [91] This deception in turn explains de Gaulle's emphasis on the negative aspect of the Nassau Agreement: "At the Bahamas, Great Britain gave the United States whatever poor atomic forces she had. She could have given them to Europe. She has thus made her choice." [92] Furthermore, even on its innovating side, the United States offer was considerably watered down. When, a few days after the Nassau meeting, Undersecretary George Ball visited Paris, the emphasis was placed on the integrationist side of the Nassau proposal,[93] which led de Gaulle to make his first, unofficial refusal: "The American propositions are words only. They are merely a façade which . . . will give the United States the possibility of seizing the French atomic forces." [94]

In the last analysis, then, the September memorandum, which had made, in its words, "further French participation in the Atlantic Organization conditioned upon the acceptance of [France's] claims," was no longer valid by 1963. Already, in the spring of 1961, de Gaulle was uncertain of his position, even though the Berlin crisis made him cautious enough to postpone any further claim or quarrel until after its solution. Moreover, de Gaulle's freedom of movement was still hampered by his policy toward Europe and more particularly toward Germany as he was aware of the impossibility of Germany's loosening her bonds with the United States at such a time of international crisis. In effect, it is less

[91] Statement of Feb. 6, 1963, Passeron, *De Gaulle Parle*, Vol. 2, p. 199.

[92] Statement of Jan. 24, 1963, *ibid.*, p. 207.

[93] Schlesinger, *A Thousand Days*, p. 867. See also André Fontaine, "Histoire de la Force Multilatérale."

[94] Statement of Jan. 5, 1963, Passeron, *De Gaulle Parle*, Vol. 2, p. 200.

France than the United States government which precipitated the choice for Bonn by promoting the multilateral force. As seen by the French government, the MLF intended to solve two American problems at once: on the one hand, it would satisfy German nuclear aspirations, and on the other, it would eliminate French influence on the Continent and more particularly, destroy the effectiveness of the newly born Franco-German treaty by forcing Germany's choice between Paris and Washington. As such, it was—according to Prime Minister Pompidou—"destructive for Europe, provocative for some countries, and even perhaps directed against France." [95] But should the multilateral force lead to the creation of some sort of military alliance between Germany and the United States, the French government made it clear to Bonn that it "could not consider such a realization as being compatible with the relations presently enjoyed between France and Germany under the terms of the treaty between both countries." [96]

Meanwhile, as détente spread, French diplomacy sought more distance from American diplomacy "more skilled in exploiting a Soviet toughening than an attempt at détente." [97] Aware that she was not the most powerful nation in the world, de Gaulle's France dreamed of being the smartest. Besides, NATO had been seen as the only means of solving the French dilemma: to keep world influence while not being, in actual terms, a world power. Yet, here too, NATO was no longer necessary, as de Gaulle could now boast of "being in practical, direct, and fruitful contact with the whole world." [98] Even the race with England over the leadership of Europe was believed to have been won by Gaullist France, thus cancelling those demands for equality, as it came to be widely believed that France's colonial quarrels had proved less costly than Great Britain's European incertitudes.[99] Up to 1962, it might have been possible for France's allies to open negotiations with her along

[95] Quoted in *ibid.*, p. 242.
[96] *Le Monde Hebdomadaire,* Nov. 5–11, 1964.
[97] *L'Année Politique, 1958,* p. 336.
[98] *Ibid., 1965,* p. 110.
[99] Grosser, "Faut-il admirer l'Angleterre?" *Le Monde,* Mar. 3, 1966.

the lines suggested by the 1958 memorandum, even though procedural matters made them quite difficult. But by 1963, the French government had seemingly changed its mind: "In response to informal governmental inquiries," stated former Secretary of the Treasury Douglas Dillon, "the French have never been willing to answer as to what changes they wanted and how they wanted them made." [100] What is surprising, then, is not that France departed from NATO, but that she departed so late.[101]

## III

In 1955, with the restoration of German sovereignty and the end of the occupation regime, Franco-German relations entered an entirely new phase. The former policy of security had, as we have seen, been continuously eroded by successive concessions in the London Agreements, the Paris Protocol, the EDC Treaty, and the Paris Agreements. The only alternative left, as Robert Schuman and some of his colleagues at the Foreign Ministry and at the National Assembly had soon realized, was a policy of co-operation: security could not remain a matter for one country alone.

Close co-operation between France and Germany had long been dear to de Gaulle. During the last months of 1944, Himmler—trying to dismantle the coalition of the United Nations—had suggested to him that an alliance between their two states would enable Europe to face the two nascent extra-European blocs. Even though de Gaulle rejected this not-too-subtle offer, he found in it "an element of truth." [102] Late in 1949, he adapted this idea within the context of the debates then going on about the unification of Europe. "There will or will not be a Europe," he then said, "de-

[100] Douglas Dillon, *Hearings*, p. 59. Also, General Norstad, ibid., p. 97.
[101] See statement made by Couve de Murville, quoted in *Le Monde*, Mar. 19, 1966.
[102] *Mémoires*, III, 206.

pending on whether an agreement between the Germans and the Gauls, *concluded without any intermediaries*, is possible." [103]

These views remained unchanged during the Fifth Republic, as one of the main objectives of French diplomacy in Europe has been the establishment of a special relationship between Paris and Bonn, in many ways identical to that existing between London and Washington. To this effect, and during their first meeting at Rambouillet in September, 1958, de Gaulle and Chancellor Adenauer concluded a personal agreement underlining the terms of such an entente: in return for complete support of France for German claims, Germany would back up French positions toward NATO and Europe. [104]

The elements of such an agreement were, however, poorly defined. Adenauer, certainly aware of the French concern over the organization of the Atlantic Alliance, could not yet fully grasp the Gaullist position on this matter, as the memorandum on NATO was presented to Washington only two weeks later. Should the German Chancellor have been informed of its content, then it is fair to assume that de Gaulle emphasized that, in any case, there was no necessity for Germany to choose between Paris and Washington.

On the other hand, some of the German claims were difficult for France to endorse. When de Gaulle spoke of a "Germany as it is" as the only harmless Germany,[105] he obviously implied a certain recognition of, and satisfaction with, the status quo. Such an approval of "the facts that have been accomplished there . . . facts [which] must be taken as they are and lived with" [106] was conducive to positions which could be both favorable and un-

[103] Quoted in Massip, *De Gaulle et l'Europe*, p. 53. (Emphasis is the author's.)

[104] Grosser, *La Vème République*, p. 85.

[105] "Germany, as it is, in no way threatens us." *Major Addresses* (Mar. 25, 1959), p. 42. "One may wonder if there is someone who truly believes that the Federal Republic of Germany, such as it is, is a danger to the present Russia." *Ibid.* (Sept. 5, 1961), p. 140.

[106] Press conference of May 15, 1962, *ibid.*, p. 178.

favorable to German expectations: the tough policy on Berlin, together with the solemn declaration not to recognize the Pankow government as a sovereign and independent state were thus identical in spirit with the recognition of the Oder–Neisse line.[107]

Nevertheless, and until the Summit Conference of May, 1960, the German government was seemingly impressed by the apparent determination of Gaullist diplomacy to revive and promote efforts aiming at German reunification. In September, 1959, for example, Foreign Minister Couve de Murville declared at the United Nations that "concerning Germany, it is now . . . high time to reach a settlement . . . concluded only on the basis of the reunification of the two parts of Germany which now constitute completely separate entities." [108]

But after the failure of the Summit Conference, where de Gaulle had expected to find at long last the end of Yalta, a return to the methodical steps of diplomacy was demanded for the stabilization of the status quo until the time when a definite détente would permit a specific degree of controlled disarmament and a reasonable level of organized co-operation between East and West "devoted to the service of man." [109]

These nuances and changes, what Alfred Grosser calls "the thesis of variations," [110] were largely ignored while Adenauer and de Gaulle continued to tighten their bonds of personal understanding. There is no doubt that the treaty of January, 1963, was more a personal treaty between chiefs of state than one between France and Germany. Walter Lippmann was the first to see it when he emphasized: "The Franco–German combination today is an alliance between General de Gaulle and Dr. Adenauer." [111] It was particularly satisfying to de Gaulle since, in line with his expectations, it called for a regular co-operation and consultation be-

---

[107] Press conference of Mar. 25, 1959, *ibid.*, p. 43.
[108] French Embassy, *Speeches and Press Conferences*, No. 141 (Sept. 30, 1959).
[109] French Embassy, *Major Addresses* (May 31, 1960), pp. 75–77.
[110] *La Vème République*, p. 153.
[111] *Western Unity and the Common Market* (Boston, 1962), p. 22.

tween national governments with no element whatsoever of supra-nationality.[112]

From a Gaullist point of view, however, the signing of the treaty implied Germany's rallying to France's thesis of independence from the United States, as de Gaulle later reminded Adenauer's successor of its "incompatibility with an attitude too favorable to the American position." [113] Yet, the German *Bundestag* clearly stated, in a preamble attached to the treaty, that the Franco–German agreement in no way prevented "common defense within the framework of the North Atlantic Alliance and the integration of armed forces of member states of that pact, [and] the unification of Europe according to the patterns set up by the existing European Communities and by admitting Great Britain and other states which want to join." [114] The preamble thus measured the gap existing between a "gentlemen's agreement" and a formal, binational treaty. By promoting the formalization of their agreement, Adenauer thought that he would bind Germany to the Gaullist policy, a bond which de Gaulle believed to have directly secured from the German people during his official visit to Germany. As to the action of the *Bundestag*, it was easily dismissed as were the occasional interferences in France of the National Assembly.[115]

The treaty itself was essentially political. It was a marriage of convenience motivated by Germany's fear of a French reversal of alliances and France's need of Bonn for the promotion of her concept of European unity. The breakdown in German-American communication after two years of the Kennedy administration had

[112] For a text of the treaty, see French Embassy, *French Affairs*, No. 152, Jan. 22, 1963.

[113] Statement of July 4, 1964, Passeron, *De Gaulle Parle*, Vol. 2, p. 345.

[114] *L'Année Politique, 1963*, pp. 406–7.

[115] Such comparison between the domestic institutions of both countries is frequent with de Gaulle who once commented, for example: "The Germans do not have a good constitution because they do not have the referendum." Passeron, *De Gaulle Parle*, Vol. 2 (Feb. 5, 1963), p. 339. In effect, the referendum is forbidden by the German constitution as a direct consequence of the Hitler era.

led Germany to fear her eventual isolation in Europe.[116] But the MLF marked Germany's return to Atlantic ties as, among other things, it would have been a concrete symbol of American-European interdependence.[117] Germany's endorsement of the multilateral force meant a choice by Bonn which Paris tried to reverse by implicitly threatening the German government with a change of direction through the reconstitution of a Russo-French alliance[118] directed against a "Germany which is changing and of which we completely ignore where will go her ambitions." [119]

The Gaullist warning was made all the more effective by a parallel evolution of de Gaulle's dialectic about Germany's nuclear role. When initially asked about it, he referred his audience first to Bonn and next to Washington.[120] But as German interest in the American plan grew, the Gaullist position became more adamant: "Germany has no nuclear arms and must not have any," [121] emphasized de Gaulle late in 1965, shortly after the visit to Moscow of his Foreign Minister, whose opposition to a further spread of nuclear weapons had been signified in the final communiqué signed with the Russians.[122]

The failure of de Gaulle's German policy is thus inherent in his inability, despite the treaty and a long courtship, to influence the policy of Germany at all. Such powerlessness was implicitly recognized by Couve de Murville after the NATO crisis, in March, 1966. "In Germany," he then said, "the perspectives cannot be the same as here . . . and it is less than probable that our initiatives will make her shift her attitude." [123] The French government had previously believed that Germany had endorsed its thesis on the

[116] James L. Richardson, *Germany and the Atlantic Alliance* (Cambridge, Mass., 1966), pp. 64–66.

[117] *Ibid.*, p. 70.

[118] Press conference of July 23, 1964, Passeron, *De Gaulle Parle*, Vol. 2, p. 295.

[119] Address of Dec. 14, 1965, *ibid.*, p. 358.

[120] French Embassy, *Major Addresses* (May 15, 1962), p. 179; (Jan. 14, 1963), p. 221.

[121] Passeron, *De Gaulle Parle*, Vol. 2, p. 260.

[122] Cited in *Le Monde*, Nov. 3, 1965.

[123] Quoted in *Le Monde*, Apr. 16, 1966.

major international issues involving Europe. In practice, however, the German government and the German *Bundestag* continued to prefer NATO without France to either the disappearance of NATO[124] or even a Europe without NATO.[125]

Nevertheless, great hopes are placed in France on the so-called German Gaullists. The more recent orientation of the West German policy—its pronounced overture to the East—have further inflated such hopes. But an understanding between French and German Gaullists could only be of a short-term nature, as their agreement would be based primarily on the immediate attitude to adopt toward the United States and NATO. Even so, such agreement would remain confined within the narrow limits set up by the absolute need of the Atlantic Alliance for the security of Germany. Within these limits, both forms of Gaullism have conflicting, and sometimes incompatible, aspirations—over the Eastern European countries, reunification, and Germany's nuclear role.

In effect, Germany is at the center of the contradictions of the present foreign policy of France. Without the support of Germany, France cannot have a policy of European unity. Yet, with Germany, she can hardly have a détente with the Soviet Union unless the Soviet Union is itself interested in a détente with Germany, in which case the goal of European unity becomes still more distant. France needs German support to undo the Atlantic Alliance without remaining isolated in Europe, yet she needs the Atlantic Alliance to restrain Germany. She needs Great Britain in Europe to balance the American pillar, yet she needs Great Britain out of Europe to promote the European pillar. We shall return, in the following chapter, to these contradictions.

## IV

Throughout the fifties, the Gaullists opposed various measures of European unification for two reasons. First, they wanted Euro-

[124] Von Hase, Minister of Information, quoted in *Le Monde*, Mar. 16, 1966.
[125] Quoted in Kulski, *De Gaulle and the World*, p. 280.

pean unity as an act of self-differentiation from the United States, whereas the maximalists of the Fourth Republic often regarded the nascent European community as part of a constantly evolving Atlantic community. Second, they attacked a European union that would be constructed as a technocracy along supra-national lines. "No one accepts integration or is even contemplating it," reported the then Premier Michel Debré at the National Assembly on October 13, 1960.[126] Integration was regarded as the solution of an eclipsed nation, a solution which the Gaullists vehemently rejected.

Hostile by the end of 1957, the Gaullists nevertheless joined the consensus in favor of European unity as, by the end of 1958, de Gaulle had already given, in the estimate of F. Roy Willis, "clear proof of his intention to be the defender, and perhaps the arbiter, of the integration of the Six." [127] This sudden endorsement of the higher logic of Europe by the Fifth Republic was primarily based on the possibility of immediate economic gains. In May, 1962, the General emphasized that point by suggesting that, had it not been to the obvious advantage of France, the economic community would not have come into being.[128] The Gaullist government thus drew a sharp distinction between the politics and the economics of European integration. According to Couve de Murville, for example, the European question had to be considered from two points of view. On the political side, "the problem is to develop closer co-operation with the various governments of Western Europe," while, from an economic standpoint, "the problem is to implement the treaties that have been signed." [129]

Such interpretations were obvious departures from earlier Gaullist statements which had denied the very validity of these treaties. Instead, the Gaullist Republic claimed a leading role in the search for European unity. "We are applying ourselves," noted

[126] *J.O., Deb., A.N.*, p. 2516.
[127] F. Roy Willis, *France, Germany, and the New Europe*, p. 281.
[128] Press conference of May 15, 1962, French Embassy, *Major Addresses*, p. 174.
[129] French Embassy, *Speeches and Press Conferences*, No. 122 (Jan. 17, 1959).

de Gaulle early in 1962, "to lifting the union of Europe out of the ideological and technocratic plane onto the plane of realities." [130] And according to many, the claim was justified. For Alfred Grosser, for instance, "on certain aspects of economic Europe, the governments of the Fifth Republic have been still closer to Brussels than one could have expected from those of the Fourth Republic." [131] David Calleo even goes one step further in his evaluation: "Of all the national governments, it is de Gaulle's France which has supported most vigorously and constantly . . . the creation of a genuinely integrated European economy." [132]

At the same time, the political recovery of France helped the Fifth Republic to rid itself of the complexes of the previous regime. Where the Fourth Republic had displayed a psychology of the vanquished, the Fifth Republic now described itself as "the only stable and strong country" in Europe.[133] This political transformation naturally reduced the fears of an enclosure of France within the limited framework of a continental Western Europe.

From a political standpoint, the quarrel between de Gaulle and the Europeanists has been over what it takes to build a European community as well as over the nature of European influence in the world. As "only the states . . . are valid, legitimate and capable of achievement," it follows, in de Gaulle's view, that "there cannot be any other Europe than a Europe of States." [134] Only the states, "entities which cannot disappear," are the valid realities of Europe.[135] Other organizations, particularly those of a technocratic and supranational nature, may "have their technical value, but they

[130] French Embassy, *Major Addresses* (Feb. 5, 1962), p. 160.

[131] *La Vème République*, p. 102.

[132] *Europe's Future*, p. 54. As examples of this support, the French government backed up the Brussels Commission in opposing the establishment of EFTA, sent its best civil servants to Brussels, proposed the acceleration of the treaty in 1959, and effectively pressured the agricultural problem until it was finally solved.

[133] Speech made in June, 1963. Passeron, *De Gaulle Parle*, Vol. 2, p. 277.

[134] Press conference of May 15, 1962, French Embassy, *Major Addresses*, p. 176.

[135] Statement made in June, 1965, Passeron, *De Gaulle Parle*, Vol. 2, p. 305.

do not have . . . authority and, consequently, political effectiveness." [136]

As states cannot disappear, they cannot integrate either, so that "regular co-operation between the States of Western Europe is what France considers as desirable, possible and practical." [137] Co-operation between these states is all the more feasible since "there exists between them no kind of political grievance, no border disputes, no rivalry for domination of power . . . and [since] no one of them is linked on the outside by any special political or military agreement." [138] This last restriction obviously closes the door of Europe to Great Britain as well as to other Eastern European states. But, in both cases, "an evolution is taking place . . . which is not likely to stop. If it has not yet reached the stage when the inevitable transformation appears acceptable, that time will come." [139]

Yet, the Fifth Republic finds it more difficult to make precise how and why a European Europe could exist for itself and by itself. A timid answer as to the methods of European unification was provided, in 1961, by the Fouchet Plan. The Plan called for the institution of commissions in the fields of politics, defense, and culture, which would parallel the economic community previously created by the Treaty of Rome. Manned by national servants, these would be supervised by the national ministers in charge of these various fields and who would meet regularly and work in concert with the Council of Ministers. Finally, a European parliamentary assembly, also composed of national delegations, could "discuss political questions as it already discusses economic questions." [140]

The Fouchet Plan failed perhaps less because of its actual con-

---

[136] Press conference of Sept. 5, 1960, French Embassy, *Major Addresses*, p. 93.

[137] *Ibid.*

[138] Press conference of Jan. 14, 1963, *ibid.*, p. 212.

[139] Couve de Murville, *J.O., Deb., A.N.* (Jan. 24, 1963), p. 1631.

[140] Press conference of May 15, 1963, French Embassy, *Major Addresses*, p. 175. For a detailed presentation of the Fouchet Plan, see Kulski, *De Gaulle and the World*, p. 227ff.

tent than because of its implications. To approve de Gaulle's plan
would have also meant a tacit approval of his political conceptions
with regard to the question of the future of Europe. De Gaulle
wants a united Europe to have "with regard to the problems of the
world, the problem of defense, the problem of economic and social development . . . only one policy." [141] The General thus
needs a Europe which would be created in the image of France
and which would be small enough to have France lead it, yet big
enough to represent a reality equal in size and stature to those realities found on the other side of the Atlantic and the Urals. [142]

Obviously, the French government tends to regard a French
policy as the best policy for Europe. This, however, should not
be astonishing, given the vacuum which exists over the substance
of the European issue. To this extent, the Gaullist government can
easily reverse its European critics' charges according to which it
does not offer a substitute policy. At least, the Fifth Republic, unlike most of its partners, has made a conscious effort to define and
enforce what it meant by Europe, a European Europe, and a European policy altogether.

The Gaullists did not inherit a European mountain to be quar-
ried as the Fourth Republic never gathered within its rank a majority of dedicated Europeanists. Indeed, it is not merely France
which has exhibited much uncertainty over the sincerity of her
European vocation since the end of World War II. Other countries, from Great Britain to Germany, were guilty, at times, of the
same hesitations. The French Foreign Minister recently noted how
long a time "it will unfortunately require . . . to define even the
initial elements of a European policy." [143] The fact of the matter
is that the Gaullist government made this time neither longer nor
shorter.

[141] Address of Apr. 29, 1963, Passeron, *De Gaulle Parle*, Vol. 2, p. 275.
[142] Address of June, 1963, *ibid.*, p. 277.
[143] *Le Monde*, June 18, 1965.

# CHAPTER SEVEN

# THE LIMITS OF ASCENDANCY

## I

Traditionally, the "Great Power syndrome" has involved a search for security, prestige, and continuity. The syndrome refers to security because a Great Power must be able to ensure its own defense against any potential aggressor. It refers to prestige, since it involves "a set of tangible and psychological appreciations . . . of what constitutes 'normal' behavior."[1] It finally refers to continuity because a great power seeks to assure the persistency of its present status by ensuring itself against any future conjuncture.

In the modern nuclear sense, the Great Power syndrome becomes more ambiguous as the concepts of security, prestige, and continuity become themselves more ill-defined. Security can be essentially national only for the two Super Powers. Keeping up with the Joneses becomes a hopeless task, given the means of the Joneses. And because of the nature of nuclear power, future conjunctures become unforeseeable as they are unthinkable.

Since World War II, the foreign policy of France has tried to satisfy the syndrome by preserving a mutual satisfaction of both security and prestige within the framework of France's historical rank. Throughout the fifties, the emphasis was placed on national security, which was achieved through a complete dependence on the American deterrent as the Atlantic Alliance served to restrain

[1] Robert Rothstein, "Nuclear Proliferation and American Policy," *Political Science Quarterly*, Vol. LXXXII, No. 1 (March, 1967), p. 15.

Germany from within as much as contain the Soviet Union from without. France was then a small power, even though the biggest among them. But in the sixties, the emphasis is placed on grandeur in the name of which France demands a wider *mise à distance* between herself and the two hegemonial powers, since independence from either side requires the preservation of options on both sides. Even though the smallest among them, France now lays stress upon her status as a Great Power.

Yet, the question arises as to whether there is any difference in being the smallest among the Great Powers on the one hand, and the greatest among the small powers on the other.[2] In both cases, the Great Power syndrome is conceived on pretense—in the latter case, the pretense of prestige, in the former case, that of security. By playing one side against the other, by criticizing the American "protectorate" in order to offer one of its own, the Fifth Republic in fact risks what the Fourth Republic chose to accept: letting others determine without France the place and the role with which she will be left.

Unlike the Fourth Republic, however, the Fifth Republic may have better opportunities for diplomatic maneuvering thanks to the unwillingness of both Super Powers to resort to the use of force. As the military and political stalemate between sides increases, the French government may abandon its former search for an intermediary role—as a link or a buffer—and claim instead the part of a new interlocutor. The Memorandum of September, 1958, on NATO, which demanded a reorganization of the Western Alliance; the Plan Fouchet of 1961, which offered the political organization of a "European Europe" largely freed of its Atlantic links; the Franco-German treaty of January, 1963, which tried to promote a new *relance européenne* on the basis of a Paris-Bonn axis: these were the three steps—Atlantic, European, and bilateral—in the evolution of the French policy, an evolution which paralleled, in an opposed symmetry, that of the policy of the Fourth Republic.

[2] The expression belongs to Maurice Duverger, quoted by F. L'Huillier, *Histoire de Notre Temps* (Paris, 1964), p. 32. Quoted in Kulski, *De Gaulle and the World*, p. 71.

Obviously, Gaullist diplomacy presupposes détente. Granted détente, it presupposes that the Soviet Union needs, or wants, a new interlocutor. So far, however, the record speaks for itself. When it comes to questions of crucial importance, over matters of disarmament and arms control, or to prevent a crisis from escalating, diplomatically or otherwise, the world is more than ever rigidly bipolar, as both Moscow and Washington prefer on such occasions to manage the crisis in a *tête-à-tête* wherein they are not drowned by the verbosity of the smaller states.[3]

Furthermore, de Gaulle's European Europe presupposes that France, having convinced her European partners that she can somehow do more for them than the United States can, occupies a position of leadership thanks to the support of a tight Franco-German axis. But such an axis, blueprinted during the Fourth Republic and erected through a personal understanding between the two chiefs of state during the Fifth Republic, did not survive a personal examination by the German *Bundestag*. In effect, the satisfaction of the French designs of leadership in Europe does little to placate German territorial frustrations. Germany can still use France as a sponsor to enhance her respectability in Eastern Europe, but beyond this, it is hard to imagine her remaining endlessly an appendage of France.

At the same time, these various requirements of Gaullist diplomacy are themselves self-contradictory. For example, to use firmness toward the Soviet Union in order to promote German confidence makes détente all the more difficult, as was shown during the repeated Berlin crises of 1958–62 when the French uncompromising attitude pleased Bonn but displeased everyone else. Similarly, too close a rapprochement with the East transforms the Paris–Bonn axis into something more like a dotted line. It may even

[3] In the postwar world, there has been no equivalent of the 1932 World Disarmament Conference, where the participating states did not confine themselves to expressing the hope that France and Germany, or the United States and Japan, would agree, but tried to promote their own positions. Hedley Bull, *Strategy and the Atlantic Alliance* (Princeton University, Center of International Studies: September, 1964), Policy Memo. No. 29, p. 39.

lead to an American overbid which, if accepted by the Soviets, would mean the elimination of France from a hypothetical settlement between both Super Powers. Finally, French nationalism, the ultimate motivation of the French policy, obviously contradicts European nationalism, its frequent invocation, and may ultimately lead to a resurgence of nationalism in Europe.

In the last analysis, behind the shield of endless and countless pronouncements, followed by endless and countless exegeses, the foreign policy of the Fifth Republic still makes for a French diplomacy quite simple in its goals: to restore French hegemony in Europe by ridding the continent of the last vestiges of Yalta and by containing Germany. In the sixties, France, in short, seeks the grandeur of the twenties associated with the security of the fifties —all this with the means of the thirties. The outcome obviously might be that of the forties and, looking up to Chancellor Bismarck, de Gaulle runs the risk of going down as Colonel Beck.[4]

## II

"Is it really likely," asked de Gaulle in one of his earlier works, "that the present balance of power will remain unchallenged so long as the small want to become great, the strong to dominate the weak, the old to live on?"[5] Nowadays, the efforts by the small to become great lead to the nuclear debate; the assumed efforts of the strong to dominate the weak lead to the Atlantic debate; the desire of the old to live on leads to a debate over the nature and effects of Western polycentrism. We must now turn to these questions individually to draw the limits of an assumed acendancy of France.

[4] The reference to Bismarck and Beck is made, in a slightly different form, by Pierre Hassner, *Les Deux Europes et les Deux Grands*, Centre d'Etude des Relations Internationales, Institut des Sciences Politiques (Paris, 1966), p. 57.
[5] *Edge of the Sword*, p. 9.

In theory, France is certainly opposed to an unlimited spread of nuclear weapons, as she so stated in the final communiqué which followed the Franco–Russian talks of November, 1965.[6] Even though never explicitly substantiated, this opposition would certainly derive primarily from an adaptation of the so-called "prudence argument" that somehow identifies prudence or responsibility with power,[7] thereby conceding the urge of nuclear power to those nations, but those nations only, which have historically proven their sense of responsibility. The position of the French government would thus stop far short of the Gallois thesis whose balanced deterrence, if and when pushed to its logical conclusion, leads ultimately to a neutral system where each nation, isolated through the obsolescence of alliances, is protected by the relative invulnerability of its respective deterrence.[8]

In practice, however, France somewhat scornfully rejects any treaty which would prevent the spread of nuclear weapons. Such a treaty can be regarded either as an agreement entered into by the nuclear powers not to proliferate nuclear weapons themselves or as an agreement entered into by some or all non-nuclear powers not to acquire any. In the former case, the French government emphasizes the obvious, namely that it hardly has any atomic weapons to give away.[9] In the latter case, it is emphasized that the agreement would group nations which, at any rate, would have been unable to get such weapons in the first place: "It is a little bit as if many people were asked to promise not to swim across the Channel," said de Gaulle.[10]

[6] Communiqué following the visit of Couve de Murville to Moscow, *Le Monde*, Nov. 3, 1965.

[7] Robert W. Tucker, *Stability and the Nth Country Problem*, Institute for Defense Analysis, Study Memorandum No. 5 (Washington, D.C., 1961), p. 7ff.

[8] General Gallois, *The Balance of Terror* (Boston, 1961), *passim*. For a sharp critic of Gallois' thesis see Raymond Aron, *The Great Debate* (New York: Anchor Books, 1965), pp. 120ff.

[9] Press Conference of May 15, 1962, French Embassy, *Major Addresses*, p. 179.

[10] Speech of Sept. 28, 1963, Passeron, *De Gaulle Parle*, Vol. 2, p. 218.

Rather than such a treaty, the French insist on a program of complete disarmament, the outline of which naturally depends on the evolution of their own military arsenal. So, at first, the issue was debated as a whole, an agreement on any partial point being described as serving the interests of a few powers at the expense of others, and more particularly France. "Such would be the case," wrote de Gaulle to Khrushchev in 1958 before the explosion of the first French atomic bomb, "of a . . . prohibition of nuclear tests, if such a prohibition was adopted independently of an effective and controlled disarmament." [11] But once endowed with the first generation of atomic weapons, essentially the bomb itself, the French emphasis was shifted toward the means of delivery, still unavailable to France, and disarmament now came to imply "the reciprocal controlled destruction of weapons, *beginning with vehicles*." [12] In the meantime, however, and in order not to remain in "a position of chronic and overwhelming inferiority," [13] the promotion of an independent, national deterrent force for France became both "an obligation and a necessity." [14]

Given the goals and purposes of the foreign policy of France, a national force de frappe ought to enhance security from without while, at the same time, promoting her rank within the Atlantic Alliance.[15]

[11] *L'Année Politique, 1958*, p. 388.

[12] Press conference of May 15, 1962, French Embassy, *Major Addresses*, p. 182. (The emphasis is the author's.)

[13] Press conference of Oct. 23, 1958, *ibid.*, pp. 27–28.

[14] Press conference of May 15, 1962, *ibid.*, p. 182.

[15] The value of the force de frappe can also be argued in terms of cost and technological improvements. See, for example, de Gaulle's statements in Passeron, *De Gaulle Parle*, Vol. 2, pp. 227 and 219–20, respectively. It has also been described as a means of reintegrating morally and politically the French army in the nation (*ibid.*, p. 197). Finally, the French government may have had to go further than it expected when it first endorsed the concept of a national nuclear force. The terms of the McMahon Law may have led it to believe that U.S. aid would be forthcoming once a nuclear basis secured. In 1959, de Gaulle was still referring to France's future acquisition of atomic weaponry in terms of "whether we manufacture it or buy it." (Quoted by Zeppo, "France as a Nuclear Power," in *The Dispersion of Nuclear Weapons*, ed. Richard N. Rosecrance [New York, 1964], p. 121.)

The ability of France to promote her own security is based on a qualitative interpretation of the effect of nuclear weapons. "It is quite true," de Gaulle said in January, 1963, "that the number of nuclear weapons with which we can equip ourselves will not equal, far from it, the mass of those of the two giants of today." [16] But the consequence of such quantitative weakness can be downgraded since "once reaching nuclear capability, with regard to one's own defense the proportion of respective means has no absolute value." [17] Within such a context, a nation regarded as small, such as France, could deter a nation regarded as big, such as the Soviet Union, if it had a nuclear force whose second strike capability would still permit to strike back at major urban targets in enemy territory.[18]

Arguments of this type, however, rest upon two major assumptions. First, it is supposed that the rationality of the adversary will not be overcome by his desire for expansion. To this extent, Pierre Gallois' theory of balanced deterrence confirms de Gaulle's own views of the idea of war. If, as de Gaulle believes, the outcome of war can only exist through a comparison between the risks taken and the damages suffered, on the one hand, and the profits gained on the other,[19] the threat of a crippling blow might effectively deter the adversary from any aggressive action. Yet, the argument

[16] Press conference of Jan. 14, 1963, French Embassy, *Major Addresses*, p. 218.

[17] News conference of July 23, 1964, French Embassy, *Speeches and Press Conferences*, No. 208, p. 9.

[18] Pierre Gallois, *The Balance of Terror*. General Gallois also argues that it would "immunize the nation against the destruction of its big cities" as such action would encounter a parallel countercity reprisal on the part of France. He further suggests that such forces would "neutralize to a large extent the enormous Soviet conventional structure" as large concentrations of conventional forces would be prevented by the French tactical nuclear forces. ("Nuclear Strategy: A French View," in *Detente: Cold War Strategies in Transition*, ed. Eleanor Lansing Dulles and Robert Dickinson Crane [New York, 1965], pp. 238–39.) But the force de frappe is not quantitatively sufficient to exercise both tasks simultaneously. Nor is it qualitatively good enough to penetrate Russian defenses, particularly, as we shall mention later, if these were to be doubled of anti-ballistic missiles.

[19] Address of Aug. 15, 1964, Passeron, *De Gaulle Parle*, Vol. 2, p. 231.

presupposes in turn France's willingness to choose the catastrophic option of complete destruction. From a French viewpoint, the comparison between a crippling blow and a deadly blow is obviously a negative one, particularly when France is the recipient of the latter.

Furthermore, the balance of terror argument assumes that the force de frappe can reach a level of qualitative parity with the forces of a big nuclear power. As such, it is a bet against a trend which has led to a revolution in military strategy every five years.[20] Already, it can be asked what chances exist that the deployment by both Super Powers of an anti-ballistic missile system, at least of a lean nature, might be avoided until the existing technological gap is sufficiently filled. Here, too, France is at the mercy of the two hegemonies, as an end to the détente would certainly result in the building of ABM systems that would make France's force de frappe quite obsolescent.[21]

However, the French government does not present the above argument within a vacuum. In other words, it assumes that France will still operate within the framework of the Atlantic Alliance, so that the force de frappe would serve less to oppose one of the major nuclear powers than to operate as a *parachute de secours*[22] and face what Arthur Schlesinger, Jr. calls the inscrutability of history. "To say," recalled Prime Minister Georges Pompidou,

[20] Herman Kahn, *On Thermonuclear War* (Princeton, 1960), p. 315.

[21] The connection between the French nuclear force and détente is not new. In the middle of 1959, General de Gaulle agreed that the *Mirage* IV-B, which was to be constructed with private U.S. aid, should be cancelled. It was replaced by the *Mirage* IV-A, whose 50,000 pounds take-off weight badly compared with the 120,000 pounds of the *Mirage* IV-B. It is possible that the problem was simply one of expense as suggested by L. Beaton and J. Maddox, *The Spread of Nuclear Weapons*, p. 89. But the point is that by so doing, France denied herself the capacity to threaten the Soviet Union seriously with nuclear retaliation on its own territory until the early seventies, when the second generation will come into being. It is then likely that de Gaulle, still uncertain of the Soviet reaction, did not foresee any détente in the near future.

[22] André Fontaine, *Le Monde Hebdomadaire*, Oct. 30–Nov. 6, 1963.

THE LIMITS OF ASCENDANCY

"that we would be unable alone to face up to aggression by one of the two big atomic powers is an obvious fact." [23] Security toward the Soviet Union still depends on the American guarantee—that is, the pledge made by the United States through the Atlantic Alliance to do whatever it deems necessary, should the need arise. As such, the force de frappe aims primarily at introducing an element of automaticity in the Atlantic Alliance. Thus, the French force would finally reduce the Americans to one single, nuclear option to face a hypothetical Soviet aggression in Western Europe by placing a French finger behind the American trigger. "No one . . . can predict the form that a world war between the major powers would take," Couve de Murville noted recently, but "what is known . . . is that its essential element would be the atomic weapon." [24] With her nuclear force, France might expect to be able to escalate—if and when necessary—a global, massive, nuclear war. In other words, it is the United States which still deters the Soviet Union from starting a nuclear war, but it would be France which would prevent the United States from fighting a conventional war.[25]

Here too, this argument, sometimes called escalation by catalysis, presupposes a willingness on the part of France to choose the catastrophic option. "There is only one history of France," de Gaulle often recalls.[26] Is it then conceivable that the General, or one of his successors, would be willing to bring this history to an end—or is it that the French government simply refuses to think the unthinkable and takes the obsolescence of war for granted as the emergence of atomic weapons has opened, in the words of de

[23] French Embassy, *Speeches and Press Conferences*, Nos. 243-A and 245-A (April, 1966), p. 14.

[24] *Ibid.*, No. 244-A (Apr. 15, 1966), p. 5.

[25] George Liska seemingly endorses the trigger effect of the French force when he notes: "The American government need not fear the trigger effect of a European force if it was actually prepared to go to the assistance of Western Europe in all circumstances." *Europe Ascendant* (Baltimore, 1964), p. 88.

[26] Address of Sept. 6, 1964, Passeron, *De Gaulle Parle*, Vol. 2, p. 239.

Gaulle, "an entirely new phase regarding the security of peoples . . . their policy and their respective reactions?" [27]

A policy which would aim at promoting a "deterrence by catalysis" might be more readily understandable. It is conceivable that the terms of a policy of deterrence are as high as the terms of its highest bidder, even if the major share of the deterrent itself is in the possession of the lowest bidder. In a modified form, this is the argument of General Beaufre, who believes credibility of the Western deterrent is increased by the introduction of an extra element of doubt into the calculations of the adversary. Beaufre adds to this a further source of benefit as he sees in the nuclear status of France—and through it, the nuclear status of Europe—an increase in the strategic value of Western Europe and a tightening of the bonds which unite both sides of the Atlantic.[28] But Beaufre himself emphasizes that his thesis is only valid provided that the smaller nuclear force remains tightly associated with the larger one; taken alone, the credibility of the former is weak since credibility would rest upon the adversary's estimate of the smaller power's willingness to take on a hopeless solution. Furthermore, Beaufre's suggestion that a nuclear status makes an area vital is not quite convincing. As France and Western Europe are not yet congruent entities, the issue finally reduces itself to an argument in favor of a European nuclear force closely associated with the American forces.[29]

Finally, if the French government refuses to think the unthinkable, namely a nuclear war where the aggressor would "inflict death only to receive it immediately," [30] it might nevertheless come to foresee the unforeseeable. In such a case, the unforeseeable is not necessarily an American refusal to defend Western Europe

[27] Press conference of July 23, 1964, French Embassy, *Speeches and Press Conferences*, No. 208, p. 7.

[28] *Dissuasion et Stratégie* (Paris, 1964). For a concise critique of Beaufre's argument, see Maurice Bertrand, *Pour une Doctrine Militaire de la France* (Paris, 1965), pp. 77–78.

[29] This is precisely the conclusion reached by General Beaufre in his most recent book, *NATO and Europe* (New York, 1966).

[30] Press conference of July 23, 1964, French Embassy, *Speeches and Press Conferences*, No. 208, p. 7.

against an unlikely Soviet attack. "Our American Allies . . . are resolved, as we know, to fight if necessary to prevent Europe from falling, dead or alive, into the other camp." "But," the General concluded, "that is not the entire question." [31] Instead, the question may lie within Europe itself.

The possession of a nuclear force, however small, gives one at first glance an undisputed advantage over a nation deprived of any such forces. "To possess atomic weapons is for a country to be in a position to reduce relentlessly a nation which does not possess any." [32] As there is a balance of terror, there may thus be a hegemony of terror as "the life of any [non-nuclear] nation is . . . absolutely at the mercy of whomever possesses [nuclear] weapons." [33] But again, there are qualifications to de Gaulle's postulate. A nuclear France would have the upper hand over a non-nuclear nation, essentially European until improvement of the means of delivery, provided that at least one of the great nuclear powers fully approves the objectives sought by France, or else provided that both are indifferent to it, an unlikely prospect if the French action concerns Europe. Furthermore, such an argument may have a destabilizing effect as it could awake some non-nuclear nations to the necessity of acquiring a few nuclear weapons of their own in order to face the increased threat of nuclear blackmail.[34] The French force de frappe would thus be all the more effective if a treaty preventing nuclear proliferation were agreed to, despite French objections to it, since it would freeze a status quo in many respects advantageous to the interests of France.

The effect of the force de frappe on French national security is therefore, to say the least, dubious. The fact is that the force de frappe has still not reached a sufficient level of military capability to make credible any one of the three different arguments presented

[31] French Embassy, *Major Addresses* (Apr. 19, 1963), p. 225.

[32] Press conference of July 23, 1964, French Embassy, *Speeches and Press Conferences*, No. 208, p. 7.

[33] Speech of Sept. 30, 1963, Passeron, *De Gaulle Parle*, Vol. 2, p. 220.

[34] Needless to say, the difference between blackmail and deterrence is merely one of perspective. The actor who is threatened speaks of "blackmail," while the one who is threatening speaks of "deterrence."

by the French government. As it is now, the force de frappe cannot deter alone, nor can it oppose, alone, another nuclear power. Nor can a nuclear France actively challenge a non-nuclear nation without possibly facing some retaliation from other nuclear powers.

In the short run, however, the force de frappe might still satisfy the Great Power syndrome. In this case, the syndrome regards as normal the behavior of a Great Power which, in the nuclear age, would want to acquire nuclear weapons. To this extent, the French bomb and the Austrian dreadnought of 1914 are the emanation of identical policies.[35] But obviously, nuclear weapons alone, or dreadnoughts alone, do not make a Great Power, and the force de frappe, which alone does not satisfy the security requirements, does not satisfy the search for prestige.

## III

The Atlantic debate is real and more than a little complex because it arises out of a real and complex dilemma: to conciliate the contradictory interests of the Allies and to satisfy the real and psychological requirements of the weaker members. The debate often centers on strategic issues as France disputes the bien fondé of the McNamara doctrine, while the United States denies any logic to the French version of massive retaliation. Yet, it is much more than just a strategic debate. In a larger perspective, it is also a confrontation of philosophies. Since World War II, the French government—Gaullist or whatever—has insisted upon the impossibility for its people "to make war, suffer from war, fight, other than for a political policy." [36] On one side of the Atlantic, the popular credo is that wars are fought in the name of a civilization;[37] on the

[35] Robert Rothstein, *Nuclear Proliferation and American Policy*, p. 15.

[36] De Gaulle's press conference, London, Feb. 9, 1943. Quoted in David P. Calleo, *Europe's Future*, p. 110.

[37] Dean Acheson, for example, speaks of the "conviction by the peoples involved that it is essential to protect their values and lively expectations which stir their deepest loyalty and devotion." "The Practice of Partnership," *Foreign Affairs*, Vol. 41, No. 2 (January, 1963), p. 248.

other, unfortunate experience intimates that they are fought in the name of nations. But in a more immediate perspective, the confrontation is one of historical vision, and the Atlantic debate which originates in a conflict over the means of best implementing Atlantic security (*what* is to be deterred?—how and why?) ends in a conflict which, taking security at least partly for granted, centers on the means of best promoting détente between the West and the East (*who* is going to do it?—how and why?).

It has become a cliché to speak of national security as an ambiguous concept.[38] If negatively defined as the lack of insecurity, it is a value "of which a nation can have more or less and which it can aspire to have in greater or lesser measures."[39] Much of the fallacy surrounding the arguments in favor of the "let's go nuclear" thesis stems from the hope that the nuclear age has made it possible to distribute evenly those measures, negatively if not positively: it is no longer necessary to have all nations equally secure; if they can all be made equally insecure, then the corollary will be one of equal security.[40]

*Au fond*, this is the reasoning inherent in the French position within the Atlantic Alliance. The main French frustration about the McNamara doctrine is that the Americans appear less insecure than the Europeans in general and France in particular, as that doctrine minimizes the risks of the use of the only weapons to which the American battleground is really vulnerable.[41] The credibility argument, according to which the McNamara doctrine reduces the credibility of deterrence by lessening the retaliation and

[38] Arnold Wolfers, "National Security as an Ambiguous Symbol," *Discord and Collaboration* (Baltimore, 1962), pp. 147ff.

[39] *Ibid.*, p. 150.

[40] In the nuclear age security takes a physical meaning as it tends to apply essentially to the physical area of a given nation. De Gaulle, however, uses it as a means to promote prestige, seen as an end as long as security is taken for granted. But when security is threatened, de Gaulle denies any metaphysics in his formula of "France being or not being France." To some extent, the colonial withdrawal which he certainly helped to achieve is one aspect of the nuclear isolationism.

[41] See William W. Kaufmann, *The McNamara Strategy* (New York, 1964). For a French critique, see Aron, *The Great Debate*, pp. 66ff.

postponing the nuclear punishment, is but the intellectual justification of this basic desire to see insecurity equally shared.

Logically speaking, the French may nevertheless have a better point than the Americans. However sincere the latter are, it is difficult to equate in practice the security of an alliance with that of a nation.[42] In the case of a nation, security is indivisible in terms of its territory and population, and a threat to a part is equivalent to a threat to the whole. Neither one province nor one section of the population can be abandoned without risking the worst national consequences. But this is not so for the security of an alliance, for an alliance, being the formal outcome of a contractual agreement, is naturally limited in time and in scope. It is a collective means to national ends, even though—depending upon the nature and intensity of the threat that caused the alliance in the first place— much latitude can be left momentarily to the institutional body of the alliance to define those ends.

Moreover, even if the security of the alliance is indivisible, it is difficult to keep it equal. Obviously, the frontier areas of a nation are more exposed than the central areas, and the urban centers more vital than the rural. But any province must be worth the same as another, regardless of population or resources. When it comes to alliances, those frontier areas are whole nations which find it obviously incompatible with their interest to sacrifice themselves in order to preserve the whole until the time when their ruins will be liberated.

The French government therefore emphasizes that the Atlantic Alliance can only be a means to national security. Collective security is in no case regarded as an end in itself. If in the twenties the French did give the impression of embracing the principle of collective security, it was with the object of preserving a status quo in all points satisfactory to their national interest. At the time of the inception of the Atlantic Alliance, the National Assembly seemed again to rally to the collective principle by demanding a higher level of automaticity as well as by requesting, later in the early fifties, a physical expression of the presence of the United

[42] Hedley Bull, *Strategy and the Atlantic Alliance*, pp. 11–14.

States (and of Great Britain) in Europe as a symbol of the indivisibility of the alliance. At the same time, however, they gave to security a rather uneven meaning as they forcefully sponsored an "eastern strategy" which would have made of Germany and part of Eastern Europe the eventual battleground of a possible war with the Soviet Union. The fact is that a declining France could only find security in that of her allies. But as the risk of war with the Soviets decreased, the position of France has been reversed so that her government is now more prompt to point out the divisibility of the concept of security within the alliance, while promoting the equality of all Europeans in sharing the pseudo-advantages to be obtained beneath the aegis of an ascendant France. In other words, a real threat to security called for real power to deter it. But as the threat loses most of its reality, so does the power needed to match it. It thus becomes possible for Michel Debré to pledge that "the French force represents a guarantee for Europe as well as for France." [43] But against whom is this guarantee?

Only if the idea of force loses its meaning can the Gaullists be justified in asserting that the question at issue is as much whether the United States wants to stand by France (and Europe?) as whether France (and Europe?) wants to stand by the United States. At his press conference of February 21, 1966, de Gaulle warned that "while the prospects of a world war breaking out on account of Europe are dissipating, conflicts in which America engages in other parts of the world—as the day before yesterday in Korea, yesterday in Cuba, and today in Vietnam—risk . . . being extended so that the result could be a general conflagration. In that case Europe—whose strategy is, within NATO, that of America—would be automatically involved in the struggle, even if it would not have so desired." [44] But while distinguishing American security from European security, the French government treats European security as a whole of which France is but a part: "Each of our soldiers, each of our atomic bombs serves Europe as much as

[43] Quoted in Kulski, *De Gaulle and the World*, p. 123.
[44] French Embassy, *Speeches and Press Conferences*, No. 239, pp. 8–9.

France." [45] This statement is easy to refute, as Raymond Aron does, by displaying the similarity of the problem encountered in trying to associate the defense of New York and Boston with that of London and Paris on the one hand and that of Paris and Hamburg on the other.[46]

But beyond Aron's remark, the question of the direction of France's nuclear deterrent must again be asked. For if European security is indivisible, it becomes all the more difficult to legitimize the acquisition of a national force de frappe whose main justification lies best in the hypothesis of an intra-European conflict.

Yet, the Atlantic debate does not prevent the Atlantic Alliance from surviving. The nature of the commitment—valid until 1969 —does not suffice to explain de Gaulle's reluctance to leave the Alliance. Nor is it sufficient to point to the commonalities which link France and the West, commonalities of which the Atlantic Alliance is the most formal expression. Nor is it even enough to emphasize the innocence of the Atlantic entanglement, the terms of which constitute—in the view of Horst Mendershausen for example—the weakest commitment of alliance that powers can enter into.[47]

The point here is that if the Atlantic Alliance is merely a defensive alliance which results from the occupation by the Soviet Union of half of Europe,[48] then it may well seem futile to a French government which regards the United States guarantee as useless, gratuitous, and/or deceiving. The Alliance is useless if we agree with the French that a Soviet attack on Western Europe has become quite unlikely. Or, it is gratuitous if the national interest of the United States dictates that this country grant total protection

[45] Statement made by Premier Pompidou at the National Assembly on Dec. 2, 1964. Quoted in Kulski, De Gaulle and the World, p. 122.

[46] Quoted in ibid., p. 123.

[47] Horst Mendershausen, From NATO to Independence: Reflections on de Gaulle's Secession (P-3334) (Rand Corporation: March, 1966), p. 3. General Beaufre also feels that the Atlantic Treaty does no more than "express very broad and .... very vague principles of co-operation" (NATO and Europe, p. 19). However, both Mendershausen's and Beaufre's arguments are purely formal and essentially unconvincing.

[48] Pierre Hassner, Les Deux Europes, p. 24.

(to Europe) with or without total participation (of Europe)—to paraphrase one of Vice President Humphrey's favorite expressions. Or, it is deceiving if the specific issue at the center of a hypothetical confrontation in Europe is ultimately deemed by the United States to be invalid in the light of what America sees as its broad national interest.

But the Atlantic Alliance was intended to be much more than a political organization aimed solely at preparing the defense of Europe against the Soviet Union. During the debates that preceded the adoption of the North Atlantic Treaty, the French National Assembly made it clear that it regarded the proposed treaty as directed against Germany as much as against the Soviet Union. For the French, the central political function of the alliance was the collective management of Germany, and more particularly a collective guarantee against a revival of any form of bilateral German-Soviet relationship.[49] The French government has now returned to this first version of the Alliance, and France has abandoned the Cold War to return to the post-World War II period. Such is the unpleasant truth which the French allies must now face: "Since the end of the cold war, since the end of the European fear of a Soviet attack, their integration aims less at strengthening the defense of the West than at protecting Europe against the revival of German ambitions."[50]

Thus, once more, the diplomacy of France is plunged into the abyss of the German problem, as it faces a dilemma which Anthony Eden has perhaps described best: "If Germany is neutralized and disarmed, who will compel her to remain disarmed? If she is neutralized and armed, who will compel her to remain neutral?"[51] But should the Atlantic Alliance be ultimately dissolved, a new

[49] Mendershausen, *From NATO to Independence*, p. 16. In *NATO and Europe* (p. 76), Beaufre regards the Atlantic Alliance as remaining "a guarantee against extreme and unlikely contingencies as well as against some new political development." In another instance, p. 85, he speaks of it as "a kind of guard rail." But he does not explain much the nature of the unexpected with regard to Germany.

[50] Maurice Duverger, "Vérité Désagréable," *Le Monde*, Apr. 30, 1966.

[51] Quoted in Hassner, *Les Deux Europes*, p. 60.

balance would then need to be re-established through the adhesion in Europe of Great Britain as a desired American "Trojan horse" which would preserve some form of back-door security. Paradoxically, Gaullist diplomacy may very well end up issuing the same plea expressed a short time ago by André Fontaine: *"Tirez nous de là, Messieurs les Anglais."* [52]

## IV

George F. Kennan has described polycentrism as "the emergence . . . of a plurality of independent or partially independent centers of political authority." [53] It is linked to the transformation of the Cold War into a "cold peace" where both Super Powers, even though they still remain privileged interlocutors, are no longer irreversibly essential.[54]

Actually, the debate over Western polycentrism is but a continuation of the Atlantic debate. Starting with the nature of the Atlantic Alliance at a time of détente, the debate soon comes to evolve around the format of European unity: too integrated an Atlantic Alliance is seen as impeding the road to European unity by preventing Europeans from assessing their own problems.[55]

The Gaullist position—as we have seen—argues for a Europe that would be neither too integrated within itself, nor too formally linked to the United States from without. Moderate integration makes it easier for individual states from the West and from the East to resume closer contacts, economically, culturally, and politically. Moderate association with the United States facilitates a symmetric development in Eastern Europe *vis-à-vis* the Soviet Union. Yet, at the same time, we have suggested that Gaullist diplomacy also takes into account the necessity of a certain level of inte-

[52] *Le Monde,* May 16, 1964.

[53] *On Dealing with the Communist World* (New York, 1964), p. 37.

[54] Club Jean Moulin, *Pour une Politique Etrangère de l'Europe* (Paris, 1966), p. 21.

[55] This is the position taken, for instance, by General Beaufre, *NATO and Europe,* p. 113.

gration in order to group Germany. It must also preserve a certain number of formal Atlantic links to safeguard an adequate management of the Russo–German relationship, or of any other dialogue that might develop—for example, between Germany and China. West Germany is thus both at the root and at the deathbed of Western polycentrism. From a first conclusion that the European problem is indeed the Atlantic problem, it thus follows that the German problem is indeed the European problem.[56]

But what is the German problem? Early in the fifties, Western integration gave its moral caution and formal endorsement to the idea of German reunification. At the same time, however, it enclosed Germany in an impossible impasse as the Allies, and for that matter the Soviet Union, were unwilling to promote the reunification of the most productive economic unit of Western Europe and the third world industrial power, with the most productive economic unit of Eastern Europe and the tenth world industrial power. The German problem is thus to learn to live with two paradoxes: the physical paradox of a Germany that would remain—to use Willy Brandt's expression—"an economic giant and a political dwarf"[57]—and the diplomatic paradox of a détente that might effect a rapprochement between the two sides of greater Europe precisely by ensuring indefinitely that the two sides of greater Germany remain separated. The European problem is to teach the Germans to live happily with their contradictions.

Inasmuch as polycentrism marks the return to bilateral diplomatic practices, we can therefore assume that it facilitates the resumption of a bilateral Franco–German competition. As Pierre Hassner has pointed out, Western polycentrism, and French diplomacy which promotes it, imply the return to a post-Versailles Europe where Russia is contained behind her frontiers and Germany is caught between France and her traditional Eastern allies,[58] the whole system being backed by an Atlantic Alliance which the Third Republic was unable to secure. Such development is hidden

[56] De Gaulle's press conference of Feb. 4, 1965. French Embassy, *Speeches and Press Conferences*, No. 216, p. 9.

[57] *Le Monde*, Oct. 17, 1965.

[58] *Les Deux Europes*, p. 53.

by the French government behind the fashionable shield of European unity. But this unity is itself denied by repeated demands for greater national independence and a lesser level of integration. It is indeed a circular form of unity where Germany, still divided, is locked in the center while the other member states are free to move at the periphery.

The danger with too much polycentrism is therefore that it might degenerate into too much nationalism. In Germany already, some elements, now back in the government, have issued warnings against "some sort of a military Treaty of Versailles" or against the resumption of an encirclement of Germany promoted, it is said, by an ill-conceived German diplomacy which "pushes France toward Russia." [59] The three possible levels of diplomatic action—Atlantic, European, and national—are interconnected, and none of them ought to be overplayed at the expense of the other. The nationalism of the weak which rebels against the hegemony of the strong is defensible so long as it does not lead itself to excesses similar to those of that same hegemony. Should France be guilty of such excesses, it would be at the expense of Europe, since only two courses would be left open to her partners. On the one hand, they could fall back on more Atlanticism where, at least, prestige is backed up by power. As Machiavelli put it, "It is not wise to form an alliance with a Prince that has more reputation than power." [60] Or they could readapt their own brand of nationalism, the consequences of which would be obviously detrimental to the position of France.

At any rate, just as the evidence of French decline could be best found in Germany, the limits of French ascendancy are also set in Germany. So far, the foreign policy of de Gaulle's France has taken advantage of an international situation particularly fluid since the last Cuban crisis. The concern of both Super Powers with internal and external problems (an elite problem, a strategic gap, and China for the Soviet Union; civil rights, Vietnam, and the

[59] The former statement belongs to Strauss, *Le Monde*, Aug. 29–30, 1965. The latter was made by former Chancellor Adenauer, *ibid.*, Oct. 8, 1965.

[60] *Discourses*, II, Ch. xi. Quoted in Annette Baker Fox, *The Power of the Small States* (Chicago, 1959), p. 180.

promise of a new "great debate" in the United States) has made it possible for the Gaullist government, its domestic basis secured, to multiply its diplomatic maneuvers. To revise a formula of George Kennan, who had himself paraphrased it from a formula made famous by Molière, de Gaulle makes domestic politics to live, and lives to make foreign policy.

At the Atlantic level, French demands could have led to a revision of NATO that might have made possible, in turn, a revision of the Warsaw Pact.[61] Instead, the French government has behaved as if there could be no middle term between integration and withdrawal, thereby seemingly perpetuating the conditions existing in the latter pact. Furthermore, as we have strongly emphasized, if the NATO structure were to be dismantled, the framework within which Germany has been contained would be dismantled at the same time. At the European level, the French government wants to promote European nationalism while preserving French nationalism. It wants a Europe strong enough to face, on an equal status, the United States and the Soviet Union, yet it needs a Europe weak enough to accept reliance on French protection. The French government wants enough integration to absorb Germany, but strives to re-create the polycentric Europe of the twenties. At a national level, the French policy attacks the neo-isolationism of the United States, whereby the United States accepts participation in world affairs but on its own terms only. Yet it follows its own brand of neo-isolationism whereby it substitutes bilateralism for the multilateral process.

The Pandora's Box which de Gaulle wants to open thus gives promise of frightening contents. Where is the focus of the French policy? Is it an old-style *politique de sécurité* aimed at Germany with the reliance on the traditional Eastern Allies? Is it an anti-British, anti-American policy, based on an alliance with the central

[61] After the French withdrawal from NATO, the Soviet Ambassador in Paris, Valerian Zorine, stated: "If NATO is liquidated, there will be no more Warsaw Pact. If NATO loses its aggressive character, there will be a similar evolution in the Warsaw organization." *Le Monde*, Mar. 19, 1966. (Only the first part of this statement was denied by Soviet Premier Breshnev at the Twenty-third Congress. *Le Monde*, Apr. 7, 1966.)

European states? Is it an anti-Russian policy based on an alliance with the Anglo-Saxon states?

In his earlier days, de Gaulle wrote of great leaders in these words: "The question of virtue does not arise. The perfection preached in the Gospels never yet built up an empire. Every man of action has a strong dose of egotism, pride, hardness, and cunning. But all those things will be forgiven him, indeed, they will be regarded as high qualities if he can make of them the means to achieve great ends." [62] In the realm of foreign affairs, the results thus far achieved by de Gaulle are—to say the least—dubious. He denies to himself what he requires from others: "A sense of balance, of the possible, of measure, which alone makes lasting and fruitful the works of energy." [63] For, in the words of McGeorge Bundy, "the difficulty . . . with the fundamental objective of France's foreign policy [to act with complete independence] is that it does not correspond to the realities of the world." [64] More to the point, however, it does not correspond to the realities of France as de Gaulle—who seemingly understands better than any other statesman the nature of the nuclear world and its implications with regard to the use of force—does not measure with enough reason the realities of France. Perhaps the General himself expressed best the ambivalent admiration of the public toward him in his own summary of Napoleon's career: "Tragic revenge of measure, just wrath of reason; but superhuman prestige of genius and marvelous valor of arms." [65]

[62] *Edge of the Sword*, p. 64.
[63] *Mémoires*, II, x. Quoted in Calleo, *Europe's Future*, p. 103.
[64] *Hearings, 1966*, p. 14.
[65] *La France et son Armée*, p. 150. Quoted in Calleo, *Europe's Future*, p. 103.

CHAPTER EIGHT

## CONCLUSION

The study of the foreign policy of France since the end of World War II provides interesting clues as to the international conduct of declining and ascending power. During the Fourth Republic France behaved, broadly speaking, as a declining power. As an effect of her decline she had recourse to two sets of behavioral patterns.[1] First, she sought to compensate for her military inferiority by reiterating demands for more respect for her dignity. This method had been paticularly well perfected by de Gaulle during the war years in London. After 1945, an occasional "no" at the Security Council, massive reprisal at Madagascar, an emphasis on nominal equality through symbolic gestures such as the number of seats at the Council of Europe or the nomination of French generals at NATO, were some expressions of this attitude.

Accompanying this emphasis on short-term preoccupations, France chose to practice the art of procrastination, as no motion at all was usually judged preferable to a declining one. As a result, France kept wavering between the two terms of an extreme choice: either to agree or to disagree with everyone. Despite statements to the contrary, successive French governments well understood the narrowness of their range of action and their impotence if left alone. Hence, the second pattern: to convince a Great Power that its continued alliance, indispensable to France, was advantageous to the Great Power as well. This we have described as the

[1] See Annette Fox, *The Power of Small States*, pp. 180ff.

161

functional arguments: The decline of France should be overlooked not only because of France's past history but also because of the functions—diplomatic and otherwise—which she could still fulfill. Thanks to an entangling alliance, France could identify her security with that of others. "Security is no matter for one country alone"—thus ran the motto of a declining France. But the larger the framework of the guarantee, the better: in other words, France, as a declining power, needed to avoid being entangled in a *tête-à-tête* with a Great Power in order to better preserve that façade of prestige already mentioned. The slow and somewhat reluctant march from collective to regional security was also meant to apply to as many of the physical interests of France as possible. During the fifties, efforts were therefore repeatedly made to include French colonies within the projected alliance, or to present a colonial quarrel as a vital conflict pertaining to the welfare of the West as a whole.

The nature of French decline was naturally due to a decline of actual power, in relative and absolute terms. In effect, and granted a few periods of national renewal, such decline had begun since the aftermath of the Napoleonic wars.[2] But two factors were of paramount importance in systematizing it. First of all, from a domestic standpoint the decline of France was the expression of a breakdown of national consciousness which had been for a short while recovered during the politics of brotherhood. Dissatisfaction with the system and disillusion with its incarnators were thus the main characteristics of an apathetic public amidst a nation without roots. France had then become a multipolitical community, so to speak, where groups and individuals showed less loyalty to the central political institutions than to other authorities: the Communist party, the Mendèsists, the Gaullists, the Poujadists, were cases in point which, at times, represented half of the National Assembly. In practice, the lack of popular consensus was matched by a lack of governmental unity and stability. The "sick man of Europe"

---

[2] One is reminded of Renan's phrase, "France is dying, do not disturb her agony."

had no family to care for the health of the patient and no doctor to try to cure it.

From an international standpoint, France suffered from a system essentially too rigid. A clear, bipolar distribution of power made it difficult to seek and play a balancing game. The scope of the Great Powers' involvement stayed limited at least until 1956–58, as Western Europe remained the center of the opposition between both Super Powers, even when Korea seemed to attract some United States power and Truman's pronouncement seemed to emphasize the over-all ideological nature of the conflict. Finally, nascent nuclear technology, still poorly understood, prevented much restriction on the use of coercive means as exemplified by the always present threat of massive nuclear retaliation.

But de Gaulle's return to power soon came to coincide with a change in those conditions. The balance of power became more volatile; it also became more complex as new sources of power, sometimes real as in China, sometimes political as in the neutralist Third World, slowly arose; the conflict became universal in scope, comprising not just the physical containment of the Soviet Union in Europe, but also its political containment all over the world, not merely a confrontation of power, but also one of ideologies, culture, economic performances, scientific achievements. Furthermore, while the Great Powers were being actually crippled by the variety of their over-all involvement, they also became psychologically crippled as the devastating nature of the power in their possession rendered them more and more inhibited in its use.

De Gaulle did not create this situation, he merely took advantage of it. But it is precisely such ability to seize the opportunities opened by any new conjuncture which made of him a true revolutionary.[3] "In truth, the war is not over. It began in 1914; 1918 saw the end of the first round. It resumed in 1939. We just ended the second round. And the war continues. The third round is unavoid-

---

[3] "I asked myself if among all those who spoke of revolution I was not, in truth, the only revolutionary." *Mémoires*, II, 172. Quoted in Calleo, *Europe's Future*, p. 116.

able." [4] When he saw in Germany the main threat, de Gaulle went to Russia, the traditional ally—("Between France and Russia, there is no object of direct confrontation.") [5] When the nature of the threat moved more obviously to the East, de Gaulle moved more obviously to the West as he asked that "the enlightened generosity" of the United States "be extended to the realm of defense." [6] But as the international situation regained more stability, de Gaulle sought to move away from both the East and the West and to enhance his own international position by playing off one side against the other, whenever possible. He now looks toward China, "an empire that is indestructible, ambitious, and deprived of everything," and once more speaks of the possibility that a new conjuncture might be thereby introduced.[7]

Yet, the revival of French diplomacy could not have been undertaken without first checking the decline from within. Here too, de Gaulle's success was very much that of an opportunist. He could rebuild a national consensus around the immense prestige which he had enjoyed in the past and on top of a motionless and divided opposition. The foundations of European unity laid down by the previous regime provided him with the possibility of immediate economic gains after a few minor economic changes. From without, the policies of reconciliation which others had painstakingly pursued during the Fourth Republic now enabled him to enjoy friendly relations with neighboring states. His stable domestic posture then allowed him to play one tune at a time (now economic reforms, now Algeria, now the Atlantic Alliance, now Eastern Europe) at the expense of the other conflicts.

Yet, strangely enough, France as an ascendant power still behaved as the declining France of the previous years: exhibiting the same pathological sensitivity to any possible encroachment on her

[4] Statement made in September, 1946. Quoted in Georgette Elgey, *La République des Illusions*, p. 215.

[5] *Mémoires*, III, 381.

[6] Statement made early in 1948. Quoted in Joseph Barsalou, *La Mal-Aimée*, p. 97.

[7] Press conference of July 29, 1963, French Embassy, *Major Addresses*, p. 235.

national independence, the same emphasis on her functional indispensability. But the main difference lay in her readiness, whenever confronted with the former either/or choice, to choose the lonely way. For a power that regards itself as ascendant is willing to disassociate its security from that of its allies and negotiate directly with its adversary to convince the latter that the use of force would be too expensive in terms of the opposition encountered and the benefits sought.

"There is no greater drama in international politics than the rise and decline of nations." [8] Without adequate historical perspective, however, rising and declining nations are defined in idealistic rather than in realistic terms. A declining power in April, 1958, France was an ascending power two months later. As France checked her decline from within, she began to rise without. Yet, she still remained fundamentally unable to supersede, or to resolve, the basic conflict. As such, France remained, throughout the period considered, a Middle Power, and as a Middle Power she pursued a foreign policy whose three major tenets were particularly consistent with past tradition.

*Vis-à-vis* the Anglo-Saxon island powers of the West, the position has been ambiguous. In general, the westward look of the French policy was at its zenith when the government was unstable at home and weak abroad. The need for economic aid at first and protection next was argued only as to the best means of securing them. Toward Great Britain, the paramount objective of the French policy up to 1962 was to secure an equal status with her. But late in 1962—as we have suggested—France in effect came to regard the situation as being reversed.

*Vis-à-vis* the Eastern power, emphasis was placed on the need for conciliation, but no rapprochement could be meaningful until the termination of France's colonial quarrels. Still, efforts were made in 1956 during a short reprieve between Indochina and Algeria as the French government tried to convince the United States of the need to revise the conception of the West toward the Soviet Union. "We have indeed criticized the Soviets so often for

[8] George Liska, *Europe Ascendant*, p. 1.

having maintained the Iron Curtain that we cannot attempt now to draw that curtain ourselves between two parts of the world." [9] Suez soon brought those efforts to a premature end, at least until the Franco–German treaty became a cordial virtuality.

Finally, Germany, the central European power, is the third constant of the French foreign policy, as she has remained the center of the policy of France in Europe. Early in the period, the entry of France in the Cold War was delayed by Germany, but it was then accelerated by the fear of being left alone with her; now, it is the exit of France from the Cold War which is being delayed by Germany. In between, successive French governments have tried the whole gamut of diplomatic devices to entangle her through links which have been successively functional, contractual, sentimental, and politico-strategic.

It is thus with regard to Germany that the French have kept "their feet stuck in the mud," and it is with regard to their persistent hope of regaining their past rank that they have lived with "their heads in the clouds." [10] To paraphrase Gertrude Stein, the story which the Fourth and Fifth Republics have meant to tell since the end of World War II is that of the old France in the new world, the new France made out of the old. Whether or not this is as applicable in politics as it is in literature remains to be seen.

[9] Christian Pineau, then Foreign Minister, French Embassy, *Speeches and Press Conferences*, No. 68 (June 20, 1956), p. 3.

[10] This expression (used here for different purposes) is that of David Schoenbrun, *As France Goes* (New York, 1957), p. 5.

## SELECTED BIBLIOGRAPHY

### Official Sources

*Journal Officiel de la République Française.*
   Débats de l'Assemblée Nationale.
   Débats du Senat.
*Ambassade de France, Service de Presse et d'Information.*
   *Major Addresses, Statements, and Press Conferences of General de Gaulle,* May 19, 1958–Jan. 31, 1964.
   *Speeches and Press Conferences.*
   *French Affairs.*

### Books

*L'Année Politique, Economique, Sociale et Diplomatique en France.* Paris: Presses Universitaires de France, 1944–1965.
Aron, Raymond. *L'Age des Empires et l'Avenir de la France.* Paris: Editions Défense de la France, 1945.
———. *France, Steadfast and Changing: The Fourth to the Fifth Republic.* Cambridge: Harvard University Press, 1960.
———. *The Great Debate. Theories of Nuclear Strategy.* New York: Doubleday, 1965.
Ball, Mary Margaret. *NATO and the European Union Movement.* London: Stevens, 1959.
Barsalou, Joseph. *La Mal-Aimée. Histoire de la IVᵉ République.* Paris: Plon, 1964.
Beaufre, André. *Deterrence and Strategy.* New York: F. A. Praeger, 1965.
———. *NATO and Europe.* New York: Alfred A. Knopf, 1966.

167

Beckett, W. Eric. *The North Atlantic Treaty, the Brussels Treaty, and the Charter of the United Nations.* London: Stevens, 1950.

Beloff, Norma. *The General Says No.* London: Penguin Books, 1963.

Bertrand, Maurice. *Pour Une Doctrine Militaire de la France.* Paris: Gallimard, 1965.

Byrnes, James F. *Speaking Frankly.* New York and London: Harper Brothers, 1947.

Calleo, David P. *Europe's Future: The Grand Alternatives.* New York: Horizon Press, 1965.

Capelle, Russell. *The MRP and French Foreign Policy.* New York: Praeger, 1963.

Club Jean Moulin. *La Force de Frappe et le Citoyen.* Paris: Editions du Seuil, 1963.

———. *Une Politique de la Gauche.* Paris: Editions du Seuil, 1965.

de Gaulle, Charles. *The Army of the Future.* Philadelphia and New York: J. B. Lippincott Company, 1941.

———. *Le Fil de l'Épée.* Paris: Berger-Levrault, 1944.

———. *Mémoires de Guerre.* 3 vols. Paris: Librairie Plon, 1954, 1956, 1959.

de la Gorce, Paul-Marie. *The French Army.* New York: Praeger, 1963.

Delmas, Claude; Carpentier, General Marcel; Gallois, General Pierre–M.; and Faure, Maurice. *L'Avenir de l'Alliance Atlantique.* Paris: Berger-Levrault, 1961.

Diebold, William, Jr. *The Schuman Plan; A Study in Economic Co-operation, 1950–1959.* New York: Praeger (for the Council on Foreign Relations), 1959.

Duverger, Maurice. *La Cinquième République.* Paris: Presses Universitaires de France, 1963.

Earle, Edward Mead. *Modern France.* Princeton: Princeton University Press, 1951.

Elgey, Georgette. *La République des Illusions.* Vol. 1, 1945–1951. Paris: Fayard, 1965.

Fauvet, Jacques. *La France Déchirée.* Paris: Fayard, 1957.

———. *La Quatrième République.* Paris: Fayard, 1959.

Fontaine, André. *L'Alliance Atlantique à l'Heure du Dégel.* Paris: Calmann-Lévy, 1959.

Fougeyrollas, Pierre. *La Conscience Politique dans la France Contemporaine.* Paris: Denoël, 1963.

Fox, Annette Baker. *The Power of Small States—Diplomacy in World War II.* Chicago: University of Chicago Press, 1957.

Freymond, Jacques. *The Saar Conflict, 1945–1955.* London: Stevens; New York, F. A. Praeger, 1960.

Furniss, Edgar S. *France, Troubled Ally: de Gaulle's Heritage and Prospect.* New York: Praeger, 1959.

———. *The Office of the Premier in French Foreign Policy-making: an Application of Decision-making Analysis.* Princeton: Princeton University, Foreign Policy Analysis Series, No. 5, 1954.

———. *Weaknesses in French Foreign Policy-making.* Princeton: Princeton University, Center of International Studies, Memorandum No. 5, 1954.

Gallois, Pierre. *The Balance of Terror.* Boston: Houghton and Mifflin, 1961.

Grosser, Alfred. *La IV^e République et sa Politique Extérieure.* Paris: Armand Colin, 1961.

———. *La Politique Extérieure de la V^e République.* Paris: Editions du Seuil, 1965.

Haas, Ernst. *The Uniting of Europe; Political, Social, and Economic Forces.* Stanford, Calif.: Stanford University Press, 1958.

Haines, C. Grove. *European Integration.* Baltimore: Johns Hopkins University Press, 1957.

Halévy, Dominique. *Contre la Bombe.* Paris: Les Editions de Minuit, 1960.

Hassner, Pierre. *Les Deux Europes et les Deux Grands.* Paris: Centre d'Etudes des Relations Internationales, Institut des Sciences Politiques, 1966.

Hoffmann, Stanley, *et al. In Search of France.* Cambridge: Harvard University Press, 1963.

Ismay, Lord. *NATO, the First Five Years, 1949–54.* Paris: NATO, 1954.

Kaufman, William W. *The McNamara Strategy.* New York: Harper and Row, 1964.

Kennan, George. *Russia, the Atom, and the West.* New York: Harper, 1958.

Kitzinger, U. W. *The Economics of the Saar Question.* Oxford: Oxford University Press, 1958.

Kulski, W. W. *De Gaulle and the World. The Foreign Policy of the Fifth French Republic.* Syracuse, New York: Syracuse University Press, 1966.

Lacouture, Jean. *De Gaulle.* Paris: Editions du Seuil, 1965.

Leites, Nathan. *Images of Power in French Politics.* RAND Memorandum, RM/2954/RC, June, 1962.

———, and de la Malène, Christian. *Paris from EDC to WEU.* RAND Memorandum, RM/1668/RC, March, 1956.

Lippmann, Walter. *Western Unity and the Common Market*. Boston: Atlantic-Little, Brown, 1962.

Liska, George. *Europe Ascendant. The International Politics of Unification*. Baltimore: Johns Hopkins Press, 1964.

Macridis, Roy C. (ed.). *De Gaulle, Implacable Ally*. New York and London: Harper and Row, 1966.

————, and Brown, Bernard E. *The De Gaulle Republic. Quest for Unity*. Homewood, Illinois: The Dorsey Press, Inc., 1960.

Massip, Roger. *De Gaulle et l'Europe*. Paris: Flammarion, 1963.

Mauriac, François. *Bloc Notes, 1952–1957*. Paris: Flammarion, 1958.

————. *De Gaulle*. New York: Doubleday and Co., 1966.

Moch, Jules. *Histoire du Réarmement Allemand Depuis 1950*. Paris: Robert Laffont, 1965.

Northedge, Frederick. *British Foreign Policy. The Process of Readjustment, 1945–1961*. New York: Praeger, 1962.

Nutting, Anthony. *Europe Will Not Wait: A Warning and a Way Out*. London: Hollis and Carter, 1960.

Osgood, Robert E. *NATO, the Entangling Alliance*. Chicago: University of Chicago Press, 1962.

Passeron, André. *De Gaulle Parle, 1958–1962*. Paris: Plon, 1962.

————. *De Gaulle Parle, 1962–1966*. Paris: Fayard, 1966.

Patrick, Charles William. *The American Press and the European Army, 1950–1954*. Ambilly-Annemasse: Imprimerie des Presses de Savoie, 1965.

Pickles, Dorothy. *The Uneasy Entente: French Foreign Policy and Franco-British Misunderstandings*. London: Oxford University Press, 1966.

Pinder, John. *Europe against de Gaulle*. London: Pall Mall Press, 1963.

Price, Harry B. *The Marshall Plan and Its Meaning*. Ithaca, New York: New York University Press, 1955.

Puchala, Donald J. (ed.). *Western European Attitudes on International Problems, 1952–1961*. Research Memo No. 1, Yale University, January, 1964.

Reynaud, Paul. *The Foreign Policy of Charles de Gaulle*. New York: The Odyssey Press, 1964.

Richardson, James L. *Germany and the Atlantic Alliance. The Interaction of Strategy and Politics*. Cambridge: Harvard University Press, 1966.

Robertson, Arthur H. *The Council of Europe. Its Structure, Functions and Achievements*. London: F. A. Praeger, 1956.

Rosecrance, Richard N. *The Dispersion of Nuclear Weapons*. New York and London: Columbia University Press, 1964.

Rouanet, Pierre. *Mendès-France au Pouvoir, 1954–1955.* Paris: Robert Laffont, 1965.

Scheinman, Lawrence. *Atomic Energy Policy in France under the Fourth Republic.* Princeton, N.J.: Princeton University Press, 1965.

Schlesinger, Arthur, Jr. *A Thousand Days.* Boston: Houghton Mifflin Co., 1966.

Schmitt, Hans A. *The Path to European Union, from the Marshall Plan to the Common Market.* Baton Rouge: Louisiana State University, 1962.

Schuman, Frederick L. *War and Diplomacy in the French Republic; an Inquiry into Political Motivations and the Control of Foreign Policy.* New York and London: McGraw-Hill Book Co., 1931.

Tournoux, Jean Raymond. *Secrets d'Etat.* Paris: Plon, 1960.

Tucker, Robert W. *Stability and the Nth Country Problem.* Washington, D.C.: Institute for Defense Analysis, Study Memorandum No. 5, 1961.

U.S., Department of State, *The Geneva Conference of Heads of Government,* International Organization and Conference Series I, No. 29. Washington, D.C.: Department of State Publication 6046, 1955.

Van der Beugel, Ernst H. *From Marshall Aid to Atlantic Partnership —European Integration as a Concern of American Foreign Policy.* Amsterdam–London–New York: Elsevier Publishing Company, 1966.

Viorst, Milton. *Hostile Allies: FDR and Charles de Gaulle.* New York: Macmillan, 1965.

Werth, Alex. *France, 1940–1955.* London: Readers Union, 1957.

Williams, Philip. *Politics in Post-War France, Parties and the Constitution in the Fourth Republic.* London and New York: Longmans, Green, 1954.

Willis, Frank Roy. *France, Germany, and the New Europe, 1945–1963.* Stanford, Calif.: Stanford University Press, 1965.

———. *The French in Germany, 1945–1949.* Stanford, Calif.: Stanford University Press, 1962.

Wolfers, Arnold. *Britain and France between the Two Wars; Conflicting Strategies of Peace since Versailles.* New York: Harcourt, Brace, and Co., 1940.

Zurcher, Arnold J. *The Struggle to Unite Europe, 1940–1958.* Washington Square: New York University Press, 1958.

# INDEX

*Designed by Gerard Valerio*
*Composed in Janson Linotype by The Colonial Press Inc.*
*Printed on 60 lb. P&S, R by The Colonial Press Inc.*
*Bound in G.S.B. #535 by The Colonial Press Inc.*